EXHAUSTED

WHY TEACHERS ARE SO TIRED
AND WHAT THEY CAN DO ABOUT IT

PAUL MURPHY

WWW.TEACHERHABITS.COM

Exhausted Copyright © 2017

by Paul Murphy

Disclaimer

No part of this publication may be reproduced or transmitted in any form by any means, mechanical or electronic, including photocopying or recording, or by any information storage and retrieval system, or transmitted by email without permission in writing from the copyright holder.

While all attempts have been made to verify the information provided in this publication, the author does not assume responsibility for errors, omissions, or contrary interpretations of the subject matter herein. He is, after all, only human.

The book is for entertainment purposes only. The views expressed are those of the author alone, and should not be taken as expert advice, instruction, or commands. As unfair as it sometimes feels, the reader is responsible for his or her own actions.

Adherence to all applicable laws and regulations, including international, federal, state, and local governing professional licensing, business practices, advertising, and all other aspects of doing business in the US, Canada, or any other jurisdiction is the sole responsibility of the reader.

Neither the author nor the publisher assumes any responsibility or liability whatsoever on behalf of the purchaser or reader of these materials.

Any perceived slight of any individual or organization is unintentional. Except for Tiger Woods and John Edwards. That stuff's on purpose, and they deserve it.

CONTENTS

More

"And when you ask them, 'How much should we give?'
Ooh, they only answer, 'More, more, more!'"

"Fortunate Son"
Creedence Clearwater Revival

Are you tired after teaching?

Better question: When was the last time you *weren't* tired after teaching?

If you're like most teachers, being tired at the end of the day is a way of life. We've become so accustomed to it that it's hard to imagine how things could be any different. We get through our mornings with coffee, our afternoons with Diet Coke, and the ends of our school days with the iron strength of our will. We leave the building exhausted, having given so much at work that there's little left over for our families or even ourselves.

Our non-teacher friends have a hard time understanding how we could be so tired. After all, we're not building houses, working under tight deadlines, competing with co-workers to sell the most widgets, or slaving in some ultra-competitive office with an unreasonable boss breathing down our necks. We work with kids! Our contracts require seven-hour days! We have a lot of control over our own schedules! We have summer vacation! Some teachers have these thoughts themselves and wonder what's wrong with them. How in the world can we be so exhausted?

All teachers I know wish they had more energy at the end of the day. They want to give their best to their families, instead of whatever remains after another draining day in the classroom. They want to exercise, enjoy a hobby, play with their kids, and talk with their spouses. They dream of reclaiming the vitality of their youth and actually spending a Friday night somewhere other than asleep on their couches. Some of them even wish they had more energy for checking papers and planning more engaging lessons.

They vow to go to bed earlier, to say no to additional responsibilities, to exercise and get in better shape, to eat healthier, and to not let stress get to them, all in the hopes that next year they won't be so worn out. And yet, by the time the holidays roll around, they're whipped again, wondering how in the world they'll find the energy to finish the school year.

When you ask teachers what makes them so tired, you get a lot of answers. Some cite large class sizes or a lack of administrative support. Others say they're asked to do too many things. Many teachers bemoan the lack of stability in their careers, which forces them to adapt to changing environments and learn new standards and curriculums year after year. Still others pin their fatigue on the stress they feel over the constant pressure to increase student achievement and the guilt weighing on them for not doing more. Some teachers can't explain it at all; they just know they're pooped.

Although commonsense advice like sleeping eight hours a night is easily said, getting that sleep if you're a teacher is a legitimate challenge. It's one thing to promise to check fewer papers so you have more time to detach from work at night, but it's another to find ways to cut back and still feel like you're doing a good job. Saying no to your principal sounds simple, but how will you handle her disappointment? Will you feel guilty when your colleagues are serving on multiple committees, attending after-school events, and running a club for high-needs students while you sit on your deck sipping margaritas?

Many factors contribute to teacher exhaustion. What tires you out may not impact teachers at another school at all. But there are aspects of a teacher's job — *every* teacher's job — that are less noticeable, but just as exhausting. In many ways, the job of a teacher today is designed to wear you out.

For years, we've been told that the way to fix education is for teachers to do more. More training, more meetings, more days added to the calendar, more time on task, more dedication, more evaluations (so that districts can get rid of more teachers), more testing, more expectations, always more. What we've gotten is more exhaustion, more burnout, more attrition, more unfilled positions, more unqualified people in front of our students, and more young people than ever before deciding they don't want to be teachers.

Doing more hasn't worked. This book will give you permission to do less. It will show how doing less is better for you, but also better for the district that employs you, the parents who trust you with their children, the students in your classroom, and the people you care about most. If we hope for an improved education system, we must first ensure that the people inside of it are well-rested, healthy, and happy. Unfortunately, there is no movement to address the problem of teacher exhaustion and burnout. Society continues to expect more. So teachers must save themselves. To be at their best in the classroom, teachers must be at their best outside of it.

This book has two parts. In part one you'll learn what makes teachers so tired. Some factors — a lack of sleep, too much work, and stress — you already know. This book won't spend much time on these well-worn topics. Instead, I'll focus more on the inherently insidious aspects of your chosen profession, those things you do every day without even thinking about them that quietly chip away at your energy until there's none left. You'll learn why even good days with students tire you out. You'll see what teachers have in common with doctors, Major League Baseball managers, and parole boards. You'll understand the parallels between Tiger Woods's infidelity and your late-night snacking. You'll relate Jeb Bush's failure in the 2016 Presidential primaries to your own fatigue. And long-distance runners, one of the world's greatest weightlifters, and a Stanford psychologist will help you understand the powerful influence your mind has on your body.

Part two of this book will give you the solutions you're looking for. You'll see what teachers can learn from baristas, what supermarket layouts can teach us about the dangers of decision-making, why AC/DC doesn't belong in your classroom, and what an insurance agent's plane crash can teach us about the power of our beliefs. By the time you finish this book, you'll know why you're so tired all the time, and you'll have the tools to do something about it.

PART ONE:

WHY TEACHERS ARE SO TIRED

Are Teachers Really That Tired?

"When people tell you something's wrong or doesn't work for them, they are almost always right."

Neil Gaiman

Ask a teacher if she's tired at the end of the day and you'll likely be told some variant of what Erine Ames, a 28-year veteran teacher in Southern California, told me when I posed the question to my blog readers. "Of course I'm tired," she said, as if it were silly to even ask.

Ms. K., a second-grade teacher with 22 years of experience, agreed. "I'm exhausted, and every weekend I spend at least one day in my pajamas. I catch up on sleep and attempt to not leave the house...or if I do, not drive. I am working against feeling burned out all the time."

Diane León, who's taught for eleven years in New Mexico said, "I am tired beyond belief, and I feel like work never ends."

A young teacher from Saskatchewan, Canada, told me, "I have only been teaching for two years now, but this year seems more exhausting than last. I often feel tired and unmotivated because of it."

Amy, a second-grade teacher in Colorado, said, "I feel that I'm always tired. I get extremely tired in October and April. I love my students, and I have a really good class this year, but I'm done and ready for a break. I was so tired that I ended up missing out on Easter dinner. I was too tired to make the drive and wanted some peace and quiet."

In February of 2017, I wrote an article on my Teacher Habits blog after reading Emma Seppälä's excellent book, *The Happiness Track*. Seppälä writes about what makes people so tired in a world that has largely moved on from the back-breaking physical labor of our past. Reading it, I couldn't help but make the connection between what her research revealed and what I felt as a teacher. That article, titled "Why Teachers Are So Tired," struck a nerve. So many people read it that the traffic repeatedly crashed my web site. Two months later, after the post was discovered by a few influential people in education and shared with their followers, my site received more than one million visitors over the course of 10 days, almost all of them the result of that blog post. A lot of teachers wanted to understand why they were tired all the time.

The answer, in a word, is stress. Teachers are incredibly stressed out people, especially when they're at work. And because our culture's tendency to demand more of educators, that stress is on the rise. In 1985, 36 percent of teachers reported feeling great stress at least several days a week. Today, that number is 51 percent. Only doctors report higher levels of stress on the job.

The costs are high. A recent study by the U.S. Department of Education found that 10 percent of new teachers don't return for a second year. Nearly one in five new teachers are gone within five years. Many young people, perhaps persuaded by honest veteran teachers or by what they see on social media, won't even entertain the thought of teaching. Between 2009 and 2014, enrollments in teacher preparation programs fell by 35 percent in the U.S., reducing the supply of available teachers by nearly a quarter-million.

While the available data reveal a stressed out teaching corps, determining how many educators are exhausted and how often they feel that way is more difficult. Lacking hard data, we're left to speculate on how widespread teacher fatigue is, based on anecdotal reporting. We have to listen to what teachers are telling us. Before you dismiss such reporting as unscientific, consider what Harvard psychologist Dan Gilbert has to say.

Gilbert's book, *Stumbling on Happiness*, is about how badly people predict what will make them happy in the future. He makes the strong case that it's the fault of our imaginations, which tend to both fill in and leave out important details.

If I were thinking about becoming an astronaut, for example, I would imagine what that job would be like. I'd pull together all the information I had about astronauts from movies, books, television, interviews, and any other source. My conception of the job would be flawed because my brain would pull forth certain details but omit others, even those I'd heard about. There would be many things of which I would be completely ignorant because, like all jobs, you can't really understand everything until you do it.

Were I to imagine what it would be like to be an astronaut, I'd think about the grueling training and years of preparation. I'd imagine the rush I'd feel during lift-off. I'd think about the unique sensation of weightlessness and how breathtaking it would be to see Earth from space. I'd imagine eating space food and floating around inside the shuttle. Because I grew up in the 80s, I'd see myself drinking Tang and maybe hanging out with a space chimp. I might picture myself on the space station operating a robotic arm. All in all, I would conclude that being an astronaut would be pretty awesome.

But I would fail to imagine all sorts of things. I probably wouldn't see myself crammed into the shuttle with seven other astronauts, the smell of the toilet constantly in my nose. I'd omit vomiting, even though just about every astronaut in space does it. I would neglect to consider office politics, professional jealousies, or the consequences of long hours. My imagination would almost certainly fail to prepare me for my fingernails falling off, atrophied muscles, and hearing loss. While the job of an astronaut may well be exhilarating, it's probably not all sunsets and supernovas.

If I really wanted to know what it was like to be an astronaut, I shouldn't rely on my imagination at all, suggests Gilbert. I should simply ask an astronaut about her job.

In his book, Gilbert describes a study where researchers presented participants with a gift certificate to a local ice cream parlor and then had them perform a long and mind-numbing task on a computer. The "reporters," as they were labeled, then described how they felt. A second group of volunteers was told they too would receive a prize and then do the same boring task. Some members of this group, the "simulators," were told what the prize was and were asked to imagine their future feelings. Other members of this group, the "surrogators," were not told what the prize was but were instead handed the report of one randomly selected study participant from the reporter group. The surrogators couldn't use their imaginations because they didn't know what the prize was. They were forced to rely on the reporter's description of how he felt following the experiment. The simulators and surrogators were then given the ice cream gift certificate, made to do the boring computer task, and reported how they felt. Simulators — those who were told ahead of time about the ice cream — were not as happy as they thought they would be. They had failed to foresee how quickly the pleasure of receiving the gift certificate would recede when it was followed by a long, tedious task. The surrogators' predictions were far more accurate. Not knowing what the prize would be, but possessing the knowledge that the reporters who'd experienced the whole thing before them weren't all that enamored with it, they figured that they too wouldn't be overjoyed at the conclusion of the experiment, and they were right.

When non-teachers try to understand the job of a teacher, their imaginations make the same mistakes mine made when I pictured myself as an astronaut and the same mistakes the simulators made when they imagined how they would feel after the above experiment. They see themselves teaching inspiring lessons to self-motivated kids, reading aloud great novels, doing fun experiments, leading thrilling discussions where passionate opinions are respectfully shared, ending work before four o'clock, sleeping in on snow days, and enjoying two months off every summer. They don't imagine all the things that make the job challenging and stress teachers out.

The lesson to take from Gilbert's work is this: If teachers, one after another, are telling us they're tired, we should take them at their word. We should, like the surrogators in the study above, believe the reporters.

17

In 2017, high school English teacher Trevor Muir stared into his webcam and reported to the world exactly why teachers were tired. In the video, titled "Teaching is Tiring (and Worth It!)", Muir lists grading papers, performing in front of students, being enthusiastic, and "the month of May," among many others, as reasons teachers are exhausted all the time. It struck a chord. As of this writing, his video has been viewed over 20 million times, no doubt by vast numbers of fellow teachers who feel exactly the same way.

Teachers are telling us they're tired.

Surveys reveal that they're stressed.

And stress causes physical fatigue.

When we are stressed our bodies produce cortisol. Cortisol increases the amount of adrenaline produced by our adrenal glands. Adrenaline is the hormone responsible for those stories about people lifting one-ton cars off children who are pinned underneath. It's the surge of adrenaline that kicks off our body's stress response.

There's an evolutionary reason for all of this. Being a caveman was a dangerous existence. A simple midnight trip to the bathroom could be perilous. Club in hand, you'd leave your cave to go stumbling about in the woods. A nearby rustle from the undergrowth would put you on instant alert and kick off your body's fight-or-flight response.

Your caveman (or woman) heart would immediately beat faster in order to rush blood to your muscles, heart, and other vital organs. Your blood pressure would spike as a result. The airways of your lungs would expand, and you'd breathe more rapidly to take in as much oxygen as possible. That extra oxygen would be sent to your brain, making you more alert. Your senses would become sharper, with your ears, eyes, and nose all working to pick up any clues about the danger lurking in the dark. The adrenaline coursing through your body would trigger the release of glucose and fats from temporary storage. These nutrients would flood your bloodstream, supplying energy to all parts of your body. Your metabolism would speed up to produce more energy, preparing you to either hightail it back to the safety of your cave, or if necessary, to fight.

When the danger revealed itself to be nothing more than a rabbit, your body would relax again. Everything would return to normal. But having quickly burned through the glucose you had stored, your body would be drained of this vital fuel. With that energy gone, you'd soon feel tired and sleepy. One of the most reported symptoms of anyone who has experienced a surge of adrenaline is extreme fatigue following the event.

Teaching isn't the same as surviving in the wilderness, of course. In spite of what U.S. Secretary of Education Betsy Devos said in 2017, we don't have to worry about bears. And although we may have to hold it for an inordinate amount of time, going to the bathroom isn't as treacherous for teachers as it was for cavemen.

But when it comes to stress, we're not all that different. The problem is that the body isn't very good at distinguishing threats. It treats them all the same. Stress of any kind leads to increased cortisol, which initiates the stress response you just read about. *Any* stress you experience during the day — a critical email, a principal's observation, an obstinate student — is received as a threat, and the body reacts accordingly, preparing you to respond with force or to run for cover. As you'll see in the following chapters, educators today are under near constant stress, a fact teacher Allison Rodman encapsulates with one of my favorite quotes: "Good teaching is like being a juggler in a circus on a plane that is on fire while trying to land on a moving ship."

While this book's chief concern is helping teachers understand their exhaustion so they can take steps to mitigate it, it's important for everyone — teachers, administrators, policymakers, parents, and taxpayers — to understand the liabilities of a stressed out teaching corps. Stress is a gas guzzler; it burns quickly through our stores of energy, leaving us physically tired. Exhaustion, experienced day after day, leads to burnout, and no one wants burned out teachers in front of kids. According to the Mayo Clinic, burned out teachers may exhibit the following characteristics:

- Cynicism at work
- Dragging themselves to work and having trouble getting started once they're there
- Impatience with co-workers, administrators, and students
- Lack of energy
- Lack of satisfaction from accomplishments
- Disillusionment over the job
- Self-medicating with food, drugs, or alcohol
- Changes in sleeping and eating patterns
- Unexplained headaches, backaches, or other physical ailments

Does that sound like the kind of teacher you want for your child?

Burned out teachers cannot be effective in the classroom. They miss more days, costing districts money and disrupting their students' learning. Many eventually quit altogether, a decision that costs U.S. districts an estimated $2.2 billion a year. Burned out, exhausted people don't make good parents, spouses, or citizens. They're more likely to make bad decisions, impacting those around them, both at work and in their communities.

Burned out teachers are everybody's problem.

Many factors contribute to burnout, including a lack of autonomy, a dysfunctional work environment, and inadequate social support. But the Mayo Clinic also lists "extremes of activity" and a poor work-life balance as major causes.

In other words, when work makes people chronically tired by requiring them to be constantly "on," as teachers are, or because workers have a hard time detaching from their jobs at night, as many teachers do, then those people are more susceptible to burnout. With so many teachers professing exhaustion and leaving education, one is forced to conclude that it's the nature of the job — and the energy teachers expend while performing it — that leads to burnout.

So why do teachers allow it to happen? If the risks to themselves and to society are so great, why do so many teachers work themselves to exhaustion?

Some may simply be unaware of the dangers and the signs of incremental burnout. Others feel trapped, unqualified to do any other job. Some blame themselves, unaware of the thousands of teachers experiencing the same thing. They believe their exhaustion is the result of individual weakness, not realizing that the high numbers of stressed out teachers indicate a systemic problem and not a personal failing.

Some teachers feel like they don't have a choice in the matter. They talk about how their districts expect teachers to work to exhaustion, often failing to differentiate between the words "expect" and "require." They fear that if they don't work themselves to death they will be punished, and their fear of consequences is greater than their fear of diminished well-being.

Others have bought into the idea that the only way to be successful is to work long hours. They have acquaintances, both in education and outside of it, that seem to have no identity apart from their jobs. They go out to dinner with friends who can't stop checking and responding to work email. They know many others who get home late from their jobs. It seems like everyone around them is tired. These teachers reason that if everyone else is working all the time, why shouldn't they? One teacher told me, "During my teacher internship, I was told that I should read Rafe Esquith's *Teach Like Your Hair's On Fire*. That book made it seem like you had to work at least 12 hours a day to be a good teacher." We've normalized working to exhaustion in our society to such a degree that not doing so makes one feel abnormal.

There are other teachers who take a perverse pride in working to exhaustion. They are martyrs, sacrificing their health and well-being to feel superior to others. They wear their fatigue like a badge of honor, a symbol for everyone to see, and proof to themselves that they're the kind of selfless, giving person they've always believed themselves to be.

Some go further. They have a savior complex, seeing themselves as the only hope for their students. One teacher who wrote me said, "In addition to teaching full time, being the District Bilingual and Title III Coordinator, obtaining a Master's degree, coaching, being a class sponsor, planning proms and graduations and fundraising, doing the after-school tutoring program, teaching Zumba for students and staff whom are not in after-school activities, mentoring for Non-Violence Works, attending at least 2 IEPs per week, sitting on various committees including calendar, discipline, safety, budget, leadership, PAC, and bilingual team, I have also helped our local union get moving toward a collective bargaining agreement. I have tried lessening my load and taking a few things off of my plate but then many of these aforementioned things will not get done, and we leave the students to suffer. I teach students in my hometown, so I truly care about each and every one of them so much that I can't just leave work at work."

I'm concerned for this teacher. Seeing yourself as the only person capable of rescuing students is a recipe for burnout. And when you're burned out, you're simply not going to do any student any good.

Of course, many teachers just have a hard time saying no.

But a lot of teachers wish it were different, and are simply unaware of what's causing their fatigue. They eat better, exercise, do yoga, go to bed earlier, and get regular checkups, but they're still tired. They'd like to change, but don't know how. This book is for them.

It's important to remember that you, the teacher, are the most important person in your classroom. Research confirms that *you* are the greatest in-school influence on student achievement. Student performance reflects *your* expectations. Students learn less when *you* are absent. *You* are also the most expensive resource in education. Most districts spend more than 80% of their money in the classroom, with staff costs making up the lion's share. Over the course of your career, your employer will invest millions of dollars to hire you, retain you, train you, and provide you with benefits. It is your professional responsibility to protect that asset. Self-care is not an option. You owe it to the district that invests in you, the parents who trust you with their kids, and the students who need you at your very best. You should not be setting yourself on fire to keep your students warm. It's time to start putting your well-being where it matters: ahead of everything else.

Willpower

"Willpower is trying very hard not to do something you want to do very much."

Pastor John Ortberg

My day starts with a cell phone alarm, an annoying jingle that compels me to abruptly turn it off. Fending off a strong desire to close my eyes again, I force myself out of bed and into the shower.

On the rural drive to school I get stuck behind a tractor. I look for ways to pass, but the road is hilly and curvy, too dangerous to risk it. I drum my fingers impatiently on the steering wheel and bide my time.

Arriving to work ten minutes late, I rush to the copy room. Three other teachers have beaten me there. I wait patiently in spite of my annoyance. Although I don't feel like doing it, I make small talk. I'm pleasant. This is what sociable people do in the morning.

When I finally get my turn at the copier, it jams on the first set of worksheets. I hold in a string of colorful words and set about the usually fruitless task of locating and removing the jam.

On my way back to the classroom I pass the staff lounge. Somebody has brought in donuts. Tempting, but donuts aren't on my diet. I keep walking.

Back in my room, there's a knock at the door. Although there are six more items to complete on my before-school to-do list, I stop and talk for a few minutes with a colleague. The conversation irks me, but I try not to let on.

Then it's back to work with just twenty minutes until students arrive. No time to check my email, even though the little green notification light is blinking on my phone. It will have to wait.

I scrawl a math problem on the board for students' morning warm-up, then post the day's agenda. It's Thursday, which means my parent newsletter goes home tomorrow. I haven't started it yet. Although I know many parents won't read it, I work on it for five minutes. Better to do some of it now and some of it later, than to do the whole thing after school tonight, when I really won't want to.

There's another knock at the door. I ignore it. It might be a student, and they know to wait in line until I come get them.

More knocking. I growl to myself, get up, and go to the door. It is a student. She's carrying two boxes of Kleenex, something I requested in my last newsletter; I guess someone does read the thing. I thank her and accept the boxes, suppressing the urge to remind her about the no-knocking rule. It seems petty under the circumstances.

The bell rings. I put on a smile, stand in the hall, and greet my students by name, trying to compliment every third kid or so on his new haircut, her new shoes, their smiles.

Your mornings are no doubt different than mine, but you likely recognize some similarities. The above may sound like a fairly typical morning. It is. During a normal morning, before students have even entered the classroom, teachers use a lot of willpower. In the above examples, there are at least 14 times when I needed to exercise some form of self-control, and this was before the school day had properly begun.

Teachers aren't alone in this. A German study found that people spend about one-quarter of their waking hours being tempted. Lead researcher Wilhelm Hofmann gave his study participants beepers, and whenever the beepers went off the volunteers reported to the researchers whether or not they were currently or had recently felt a desire to do something. Half the time, people felt some desire the moment their beeper went off. Another 25 percent of the time, they reported feeling a desire in the past couple of minutes. Urges to eat, sleep, and take a break from work topped their temptations, followed by sexual urges, a desire to check email or social networking sites, and the impulse to listen to music or watch TV.

Our abilities to resist temptation, ignore distractions, and stay on task are regularly challenged. People use willpower all day long. Teachers use more than most. Our entire work day is an unrelenting exercise in self-discipline.

Why does it matter?

Whether you call it resisting temptation, willpower, self-control, self-discipline, grit, perseverance, self-regulation, or determination, science has proven that it exhausts us.

The man responsible for discovering the connection between self-control and physical fatigue is a bearded professor from Florida State University named Roy Baumeister. In 1996, Baumeister and his associates conducted a dastardly experiment. 67 college students were brought into their lab, which was redolent of freshly-baked chocolate chip cookies. The students had been asked to fast, so they were ravenous. Each student sat down to a table of cookies and other chocolatey delights. Near the treats sat a bowl of radishes. Some of the experimental subjects were invited to eat the sweets. As you can imagine, they did so eagerly. Others, the "radish condition," could only eat the radishes. Science can be cruel, especially when you're the guinea pig.

It was quickly obvious to the researchers that their experimental design was effective. The treats were as tempting as they had hoped. The scientists watched through a small, hidden window as the unfortunate radish eaters gazed desirously at the cookies. Some even picked up the cookies and smelled them before setting them back down and biting bitterly into their radish. However, all those in the radish condition were able to summon enough willpower to avoid the temptation of biting into the cookies, which was exactly what the researchers wanted.

The students were then taken to a separate room and given puzzles to work on. Unbeknownst to them, the puzzles were impossible to solve, a standard practice when testing perseverance. The researchers simply wanted to know how long each group — those who ate the cookies and therefore used no willpower, and those who were forced to resist temptation and eat the radishes — would persist on the insoluble puzzles.

The students who were permitted to eat the cookies worked on the puzzles for about 20 minutes. So did a control group who had also fasted but had not been given any food prior to the puzzles. Those who had eaten the radishes, however, gave up in just eight minutes, a huge difference in studies of this kind. They had used willpower to fight off the temptation to eat the cookies, but that effort had left them with less willpower to persevere on the puzzles.

Since Baumeister's radish experiment, his findings have been confirmed in over 200 studies. A meta-analysis of dozens of these studies confirmed his initial conclusions. In a nod to Sigmund Freud, Baumeister coined the term "ego depletion" to describe the diminishing aspect of willpower that he discovered.

Willpower, it turns out, is like a muscle; it can strengthen, but also wear out with use. Ego depletion has a general effect, meaning that when you use self-control in one area of your life, it erodes your ability to use it in other parts of your life.

There are four types of willpower that mentally exhaust teachers throughout the day. Think of how many times you use each during a typical day at school.

Controlling Impulses

Controlling impulses means not giving in to distractions or temptations. Examples of exercising willpower in this area would be working on a report for your principal instead of checking your email. It means drinking water with dinner instead of the Coke you really want. As I write this sentence, I'm tempted to give in to impulses like looking up from my computer screen to watch the Harry Potter movie on TV, walking to the pantry to grab a bag of Cheetos, or opening a new tab to see what people are arguing about on Twitter. I must suppress those impulses in order to finish this paragraph. (I did it!)

Controlling Performance

Controlling performance has to do with persisting when you don't feel like it. Although you only slept five hours last night, you use willpower to summon enough enthusiasm to effectively teach your Civil War lesson. In spite of a sore ankle at mile eight, you power through to complete the half-marathon for which you trained so hard. As a college student, you may have had to use this kind of willpower to write a satisfactory essay, even though all you wanted to do was get it over with so you could go to the bar with your roommates.

Controlling Behavior

In order to control your behavior, you must sometimes use willpower to suppress your emotions. You use this type of willpower when you give a student a patient explanation instead of the sardonic quip on the tip of your tongue. Controlling your behavior means not slamming your fist on a desk when you're angry, or refraining from swearing when you're frustrated. It also means not acting like a fool in public when you're excited, such as when you're sitting in church and see on your phone that your football team just scored a touchdown.

Controlling Thoughts

Our brains have a mind of their own, and our thoughts are not always helpful. Using willpower to control your thoughts means making yourself think about the task at hand instead of whatever pops into your head. Teenage students might use this type of self-control when, during the middle of a test, they willfully extinguish fantasies about the attractive boy or girl sitting across from them. You might use it to stop daydreaming about an upcoming vacation while meeting with your grade level colleagues. You might need to call on it to refocus on what's being said at a staff meeting instead of imagining how wonderful the world would be without staff meetings.

Teachers endlessly self-regulate. We hold back sarcastic rejoinders, walk away from lazy students when what we really want to do is lecture them, keep our honest thoughts about the principal's latest ill-conceived ideas to ourselves, respond professionally to disrespectful emails from parents, work with students when we want to do anything but, plan the next day when we'd rather check Facebook, and bite our tongues when we'd like to drop F-bombs. We force ourselves to work when we feel like taking a break. We redirect students when we'd rather just let the behaviors go and avoid the resultant excuses and conflicts. We keep teaching even though we really, really have to pee. Teachers use a **lot** of willpower.

Because using willpower in one of the above areas affects our ability to use it the other areas, a heated staff meeting that leaves us fuming and fighting off a strong urge to pen a scathing email to our principal will drain us of the self-control we may need to calmly react to a misbehaving student, plan next week's lessons, or show consideration to our spouses when we get home.

Due to this general effect, we would expect teachers who use a lot of willpower at work to have little left to use at night. We might predict that they'd have messy houses, strained relationships, or trouble sticking to their diets. And in fact, that's what two Australian researchers found when they tested the self-control of college students at different times of the year. These students, their willpower drained from studying for exams and completing assignments at the ends of their terms, stopped exercising, smoked more, increased their caffeine intake, drank more alcohol, abandoned diets, and cleaned less. They neglected personal hygiene, overslept, and spent money impulsively. They also reported being grumpier, angrier, and more irritable.

All of those are negative consequences of depleted self-control and should serve as warnings to teachers. But you're reading this book because you're tired all the time. What does willpower have to do with physical fatigue? Why does the act of self-regulating drain us of energy and leave us feeling like we've been run over by a truck?

To psychologists, it seemed as though self-control relied on some limited source of energy. They wondered if willpower worked like a bank account. Could you save it up in some way for a day when you would need a lot of it? People seemed to believe this. Why else would they gleefully indulge their every impulse during carnivals like Mardi Gras in order to prepare for the prolonged period of great temptation known as Lent? Lent requires great self-sacrifice and tremendous amounts of willpower. Did the revelers make it easier on themselves by unabashedly scarfing down po' boys, pancakes, and paczki? Could a reckless lack of self-control make it subsequently easier to exercise self-control? One of Baumeister's graduate students, Matthew Gailliot, wondered if maybe there was something to it.

He and his colleagues established three groups to test the "Mardi Gras Theory." Each group first performed a test that required willpower. Afterward, researchers gave one group ice cream, a second group a stack of outdated periodicals, and a third group a flavorless low-fat dairy concoction I will henceforth refer to as "glop." If the theory was correct — if you could save up willpower by indulging — then only the ice cream eaters would see their willpower restored. And in fact, that did happen. Study participants who ate ice cream performed better than expected on a second task requiring willpower.

But so did those who ate the glop. At first, the experiment seemed like a failure. Indulging was supposed to provide extra willpower, but no one wanted to drink the glop any more than they wanted to read the boring magazines. It took self-control to do both, but those who had ingested the flavorless glop performed just as well as those who ate the delicious ice cream. How could that be?

The answer soon became clear. It wasn't the act of indulging that mattered; it was the calories. Specifically, researchers found through subsequent experiments, it was all about glucose.

Glucose is a type of sugar you get from the foods you eat. Your body uses it for energy. As it travels through your bloodstream to your cells, it's often called blood sugar. Your body regulates the amount of glucose in the blood to keep it constant. Glucose is needed by most cells for energy, and it's the main fuel source for your brain. The brain is especially consumptive. Although it represents just 2 percent of your body's mass, it burns 20 percent of its calories. Without glucose, your brain doesn't work very well. It seemed likely that glucose was responsible for restoring willpower to depleted test subjects, but further research was needed.

Fortunately, the world provides a convenient test group. Hypoglycemia is a condition that occurs when blood sugar is too low. It can happen in diabetics if they eat too little, are more active than normal, or take too much insulin. Since glucose and willpower seemed to be connected, researchers wondered if those with hypoglycemia would have more trouble than others self-regulating. If the theory was correct, hypoglycemics would be more likely than the average person to have trouble concentrating, persisting on challenging mental tasks, and repressing their negative emotions when provoked.

When scientists looked into the available data, they found that while the great majority of people who suffer from hypoglycemia are not violent, hypoglycemia is unusually prevalent among criminals and other violent people. Researchers also discovered that states in the U.S. that are home to the highest number of diabetics tend to also have the highest rates of violent crimes, even after controlling for poverty. Similarly, countries that have higher rates of glucose deficiency have higher rates of violent crimes and murders. One study found below average glucose levels in 90 percent of juvenile delinquents taken into custody. The risks of insulin-induced hypoglycemia are now so well-understood that many states allow it as a defense in criminal court cases.

Problems related to low blood sugar can also affect your classroom. You've undoubtedly heard that students need to eat to perform well in class. Many schools make sure that every student gets a free breakfast on standardized testing days (I guess the other days don't matter as much, he said with tongue planted firmly in cheek). This isn't just wishful thinking on the part of administrators hoping to boost test scores, and it's not superstition, like believing that student behavior is affected by the phases of the moon. There is science to support it.

A group of nutritionists conducted a study in which all students in a class were asked to skip breakfast one morning. Once at school, half were given a good meal when they arrived. The other half got nothing (and if they complained, I hope the nutritionists told them about the radish experiment). The children who were fed learned more and behaved better as judged by independent observers who didn't know which kids had eaten. After all students were given a snack in the middle of the morning, the differences in learning and behavior disappeared.

It might help to think of willpower as one of those health meters found in role-playing and first-person shooter video games. These meters represent health points, or HPs. Players start a game with a full complement of HPs and bright green health bars. Then, as they're hit by punches, arrows, knives, spears, bullets, magical spells, and the like, the characters lose HPs and the meter begins to disappear, until it's blinking red, signaling impending virtual death.

When you get out of bed — assuming you got a fair amount of restful sleep — you have a full complement of willpower. Every time you exercise self-control — from getting to work on time, to eating the salad you brought for lunch instead of buying the cafeteria nachos that smell surprisingly good today, to responding patiently to Marcus interrupting your lesson for the sixth time — it's like getting hit with one of those punches, spears, or bullets in the video game. You lose "willpower points" and your self-control meter gets shorter. Your body uses a little glucose each time this happens. You need that glucose for energy, and not just the mental kind. So the more glucose your body uses, the more tired you become.

As you continue playing the teaching game and using self-control, you continue to lose willpower points until eventually, they're all gone. Your glucose, the fuel your body needs for just about everything, is spent. Your tank is dry, and you quickly become exhausted, even though the heaviest thing you lifted was a textbook. Do this day after day, and you risk chronic fatigue setting in. But fatigue won't be your only problem.

The Consequences of Ego Depletion

"Golf is, what, five hours? You're trying to tell me that I can't go out there and focus that hard for five hours, when I've got 19 other hours to recover? That's how I look at it. So I'm going to give it absolutely everything I can, everything I have, for this five-hour window."

Tiger Woods

Imagine you're the greatest golfer on the planet, already considered one of the best of all time. If there were a Mount Rushmore of golfers, your granite head, Nike cap and all, would be up there alongside Jack Nicklaus, Arnold Palmer, and Ben Hogan. If things keep going the way they have so far in your career, you'll be the G.O.A.T., the Greatest of All-Time.

In your mind, this is exactly as it should be. It's destiny playing itself out. Given your first club at only six months old, you followed your old man around the Navy golf course in California where he was a member. You were so good at such a young age that Mike Douglas invited you to come on his talk show where you putted against legendary comedian Bob Hope as the actor Jimmy Stewart looked on. At age three you shot a nine-hole score of 48. By the time you were six, you'd been featured in *Golf Digest* and appeared on the television show *That's Incredible!* You broke 80 at age eight and won the Junior World Championship six times.

You always knew what you wanted. A poster of golf legend Jack Nicklaus hung above your childhood bed. Under the poster you pegged a list of Nicklaus's accomplishments, with the goal of breaking each of them at a younger age than your hero.

Now in your prime, you have immense talent, earned with endless hours of practice. You've separated yourself from fellow golfers through indomitable willpower. Back when you turned pro, you raised eyebrows when you told two-time U.S. Open winner Curtis Strange that your goal was to win every tournament because, "second sucks and third is even worse." In pursuit of that lofty goal, you became one of the first golfers ever to take physical fitness seriously, working out two to three hours every day, six days a week.

At 6:30 in the morning, you do an hour of cardio. After that, it's one hour of lower-body weight training. You eat a high-protein/low-fat breakfast and then spend two hours on the driving range. Then it's time for some work on the putting green. After that, you play nine holes. A healthy lunch precedes two to four more hours on the golf course. By 6:30, you're back in the gym to work on your upper body. At 7:00, it's time for dinner, relaxation, and, as the world now knows, certain extra-curricular activities.

Tiger Woods's life went into a very deep sand trap on Thanksgiving night in 2009. Woods, an insomniac, had taken an Ambien to fall asleep, and his wife, suspicious after *The National Enquirer* had published a story detailing her husband's affair with a New York City nightclub hostess, started scrolling through his phone. When she found the mistress's name, she became enraged. In a delicious bit of irony, she grabbed a golf club and chased Tiger from the house. Woods, woozy from the medication, jumped into his Cadillac Escalade and promptly crashed it into a fire hydrant a few yards off his property. In the wake of that accident, 14 other women came forward with details about their affairs with Tiger Woods. His marriage ended, his reputation was destroyed, and his golf game has never been the same.

How could someone with such singular dedication, such focused determination, such extreme grit and perseverance, and such a large store of willpower, allow himself to make such stupid decisions in his personal life? Why would a man as image-conscious as Tiger Woods — a celebrity with so much to lose — send overtly sexual text messages to a restaurant hostess, leave a record of personal phone calls to escort services, and sleep with his 21-year old neighbor? How could he possibly think he'd get away with it?

Tiger Woods exercised incredible willpower both on and off the golf course. His own schedule reveals little room for indulgences. He forced himself to practice for seven to eight hours every day, and worked out two to three hours more. Tiger was often criticized during his career for allowing his temper to get the better of him on the course, but his reactions were mild compared to most weekend duffers. Even when he chastised himself, he used a lot of willpower to keep a lid on it. Like all golfers, Tiger had to use self-control to manage his thoughts. Golf is a game of mental focus, and Tiger was famous for having more of it than others. He couldn't let his mind wander for a single shot. He once said:

"From the very first shot, the first hole, you have to be that way [full-throttle]. It's one of the things I was trying to teach Jason Day this year. The first hole is just as important as the last hole, and every shot is exactly the same. So you have the same intent, the same intensity. Nothing changes."

Tiger didn't just win, he dominated. He stepped on opponents' throats. He worked harder, was more focused, had greater mental fortitude, and wanted to win more than anyone else, and he made sure to perpetuate this image in everything he did.

In pre- and post-round interviews, he called on the strength of his will to avoid saying anything that might damage his carefully-honed image. Being a public figure, Tiger had to exercise more self-discipline over his emotions than most people. He couldn't risk a negative encounter with a fan or explode at a reporter because it would have been caught on a camera and broadcast to the world. His reputation, which he had worked so hard to develop, would have been damaged. Sponsorships would have been at risk. Millions could be lost.

Certainly, Tiger had some deep-seated psychological issues. But I can't help wonder if his remarkable self-discipline left him depleted to the point that he was unable to fight off his most destructive urges at the close of his ego-depleting days. Yes, he only had to focus for five hours during a round of golf, but Tiger Woods used willpower from the time he woke up to the time he started texting porn stars. His is a cautionary tale for anyone who spends large parts of their day exercising self-control. As teachers, there are lessons to be learned.

A number of years ago I threw a chair in my classroom. Some kids were upset. A few went home crying. Parents were outraged. My principal wasn't too happy, either. I was put on paid leave for three days. The incident took place with about five minutes left in the day. It had been a trying year and that day in particular had been extremely frustrating. Before the students left for the day, I was determined to give them a piece of my mind. As they were about to reenter the classroom from their last hour music class, I barked at them. "Go in. Take a seat. Do *not* put your chairs up."

Most did. But as I walked toward the front of the room, fuming and with blistering words ready to leap off my lips, one student put his chair on top of his desk. Right in front of me. I saw red. I grabbed that chair by a leg and tossed it to the floor.

Looking back at it now, I am positive that my willpower was gone and that my ability to control my thoughts, emotions, and actions was severely impaired. Normally, a student failing to follow (or even hear) my directions was par for the course, not something that would have set me off. But in my depleted state, it led to actions that damaged my reputation, ruined relationships, put my principal and Superintendent in a difficult position, and resulted in an embarrassing suspension.

My colleagues, who knew me as calm and unruffled, even aloof, couldn't believe it. If you would have come to me even two hours before it happened and asked if I thought it possible that I would ever throw a chair in my classroom, I would have looked at you like you had a second nose. So what happened?

Psychologist George Loewenstein identified something he called the "hot-cold empathy gap" that helps to explain. When we're in a calm, or "cold" state, it's difficult to imagine how we will react when we're in a "hot" state, such as when we're tempted, in the throes of passion, or, as in the chair-throwing incident, righteously pissed off. It's easy as a teacher to say you'll never swear at a student. It's impossible for you to imagine yourself ever hitting a child. You'd never drag a kid down the hallway by one arm. And yet teachers do. You see them on the news every year. I am positive that none of those teachers whose careers have been ruined in a "hot" state would have thought themselves capable of their egregious acts, but when willpower is exhausted, we can't know how we're going to respond.

Given what we know about willpower and its connection to blood sugar, it makes sense that people have more self-control in the morning, after a glucose-regenerating sleep, than right before a meal or late at night, when their blood sugar is at its lowest.

Consider your own experiences. Do you eat a healthy breakfast, only to throw it all away with calorie-laden dinners and late-night snacking? Are you able to get yourself out of bed to exercise before school, but have difficulty getting to the gym after work? Do you get along better with others when you arrive at school or later in the day? Are you more patient with your students just after they arrive or just before lunch? If you think back to your own regrettable acts, you will likely find that many of them took place when you hadn't eaten for a number of hours or when you were low on sleep.

That's not a coincidence. Researchers have discovered something they call the "morning morality effect," which is partly the result of declining self-control as our stores of willpower are exhausted throughout the day. Psychologist Mark Muraven found a connection between using self-discipline to control your mood at work and increased alcohol consumption at night. A stressed out work day also makes it more likely that you'll cheat on your diet when you get home. More than one study has found that as the day goes on, we're more likely to engage in immoral behavior such as lying or stealing. Another study found that resisting temptation leads to a higher likelihood of unethical behavior when tempted again.

The morning morality effect explains why you're able to resist donuts in the lounge before school, but give in to temptation if there are any left at two o'clock. It's why even though you show admirable restraint by eating a salad for lunch, you wolf down four slices of pizza for dinner. When your willpower is gone, your blood sugar is low. You crave sweets at the same time your ability to say no to them is at its weakest. No wonder teachers struggle to stick to their diets.

I was talking with a parent last year. Her child had been a model student of mine, and I made some comment to that effect. The mom smiled and said she'd always heard that from her daughter's teachers. But then she shared that her girl wasn't such an angel at home. "And when I asked her why all her teachers said such good things about her but she was so sassy to me, she said, 'Mom, I'm good all day at school. I don't have any energy left to be good at home.'"

Former Chancellor of Washington, D.C. public schools, Michelle Rhee, once told a group of teachers about an incident from her first year of teaching.

"I didn't have very good classroom management in my first year of teaching. And so I was trying every single management technique that I could. Some of them really not so good. But I remember the day that we were particularly rowdy, and we had to head down for lunch. My class was very well known in the school because you could hear them traveling everywhere because they were so out of control. And so I thought, 'OK, they're particularly amped up today, so I got to do something about it.' So, I decided, 'OK, kids, we are going to do something special today.' I lined everybody up, and I was like, 'Sshh, gotta be really quiet on our way down to the cafeteria.' And then, I took little pieces of masking tape and put them on everybody's lips. And I was like, 'You can't break the seal. Don't move your lips.' I put them on all the lips, and we're going down the hallway. I was like, 'My gosh, this works so well.' And we get down to the cafeteria. They're all lined up outside the cafeteria. I was like, 'Take the tape off.' And I realized that I had not told the kids to lick their lips beforehand. So the skin is coming off their lips and they're bleeding. I had a class of 35 kids who were crying and other teachers are walking by."

What Rhee failed to mention — and what she likely still doesn't realize — is the effect depleted willpower had on her decision-making. Note that in her story, Rhee talks about how she lacked classroom management skills. As any teacher who has shared that struggle knows, poor classroom management leads to intensely negative emotions like frustration, feelings of inadequacy, embarrassment, and anger. Teachers who don't have control of their classes experience tremendous stress, and that stress uses energy. These teachers must also use an incredible amount of energy-sapping willpower. Saying "Ok, kids, we are going to do something special today," when what Rhee really wanted to say was something far more critical took considerable self-control. You can sense how hard she's fighting off the temptation to really let her kids have it, and you know this was a daily, if not hourly, battle.

That this event took place right before lunch is telling. Other than the end of the school day, there is probably no more dangerous time for a stressed teacher. The willpower that Rhee started her day with was gone, her breakfast was hours in the past, and her glucose had run dry. Stressed out, hungry, frustrated, and worried about what others would think of her and her rowdy class as they moved down the hall, Rhee did something I am sure she never imagined herself capable of doing.

Diminished willpower means lower blood sugar, which means physical fatigue, reduced impulse control, bingeing behavior, and other poor decision-making.

- We eat the whole bag of Cheetos instead of stopping at a reasonable amount (maybe that's just me).

- We take the Hershey's Kisses offered at the meeting after school.

- We watch three hours of Netflix, neglecting the math tests in our bag that we planned to grade.

- We don't go the gym like we intended to.

- We let loose with a careless remark that we'd normally suppress and now our wife hates our guts (probably because she's also depleted).

- We snarkily reply to a colleague's email and regret it the next morning when our willpower has been restored by a good night's rest.

Unfortunately, unlike video game characters, we do not have meters floating above our heads telling us how much willpower we have left. There is no blinking red bar or other obvious indicator letting us know that we're in danger of running out and are at heightened risk for making awful decisions. There is, however, one subtle sign that signifies our ability to ward off temptation is at risk of expiring. Research by Kathleen Vohs, a psychologist at the University of Minnesota, found that depleted persons react more strongly than normal to stimuli. Their emotions are closer to the surface.

When you're low on willpower, you might, for example, be more disturbed by a story on the six o'clock news than usual. A melodramatic, emotionally manipulative scene in a movie may instead feel poignant and sincere; you might even shed a tear. Carlos Mencia will seem funny to you, even though you previously claimed he was a talentless joke-stealer. In one study, ice-cold water felt more painful to the ego-depleted than those who hadn't expended willpower. You might overreact to something your spouse says. Hell, you might even throw a chair in your classroom. Your emotions are harder to suppress when your willpower is gone. If you find yourself laughing at things that aren't that funny, getting angry at things you'd normally brush off, or behaving like an asshole when you don't typically exhibit assholish behavior, then you've probably burned through your supply of willpower.

Desires will also be amplified. You'll be more likely to give in to cravings. Studies show that you'll drink more alcohol and eat more food in a depleted state. One study found that depleted people have a stronger urge to open a gift-wrapped present. In another experiment, depleted participants had a stronger craving for additional cookies after eating one. And if you're Tiger Woods, you may have a hard time reminding yourself of your marriage vows when in the presence of an attractive waitress or home alone with the phone number of an escort service at your fingertips.

There are usually two ways video game characters replenish their health bars. They either ingest something (food, health packs) or they sleep. The same things work for willpower. To quickly regain self-control, anything with sugar will do. But you'll be happier with the numbers on the scale if you eat healthier food with lower glycemic indices. Although sugar is used in the laboratory because of its fast-acting properties, almost anything you eat will provide glucose to your body and restore your willpower. By eating low-glycemic foods, you'll avoid the spike and crash cycles high-sugar foods can cause. You'll stay full longer and maintain willpower over a greater length of time.

The second way to replenish your willpower is to sleep. Sleeping regenerates your glucose levels. Be sure you're getting enough. In one study, those who slept just twenty minutes less than another group showed a greater likelihood of engaging in unethical behavior. The researchers attributed this to lower glucose levels. Try to get at least seven hours each night.

Understanding the connection between willpower, glucose, and fatigue leads to some important considerations. First, teachers should try to avoid making any significant decisions during times their willpower is likely to be depleted. Breech contentious issues with your principal in the morning or after lunch, not at the end of the day. Wait until tomorrow morning to reply to rude emails instead of firing off a response before you go home. If you need to have a hard conversation with a parent, have it before school instead of after.

Remember:

- You have a limited supply of willpower.

- You use the same store of willpower for everything.

- You lose willpower even if you ultimately give in to temptation. It's the exercise of self-control that is depleting, not whether or not you win the battle.

- When you use up your willpower, it's gone until it can be replenished.

- Using willpower uses glucose, which leads to fatigue and makes it more likely you'll make poor decisions.

- The only ways to replenish your supply of willpower are to eat and to sleep.

Teachers face enormous challenges in maintaining high energy levels each day. Because we spend so much effort fighting off temptations, ignoring distractions, and using willpower to control our performance, thoughts, behavior, and impulses, we often find ourselves exhausted at day's end. But those are not the only ways teachers use willpower. Science has found that we use willpower when doing something teachers do hundreds of times each day. In the next chapter, you'll learn how the simple act of deciding makes you tired, and how making decisions when you're low on willpower can lead to disastrous consequences.

The Deciders

"In my long political career, most of the mistakes I made, I made when I was too tired, because I tried too hard and worked too hard. You make better decisions when you're not too tired."

Bill Clinton

On April 18, 2006, President George W. Bush stood in the Rose Garden and defended his Secretary of Defense, Donald Rumsfeld, from calls for his resignation. Bush famously said, "I hear the voices, and I read the front page, and I know the speculation. But I'm the decider, and I decide what's best."

As teachers, we know the feeling. We read the criticism. We hear the voices of policymakers, education reformers, administrators, parents, colleagues, and our students. Legislators tell us through their words and actions just what we should be doing in our classrooms. Education reformers try to influence our decisions through think tanks, white papers, and social media. Administrators carry around checklists of effective teaching techniques and observe us to see if we're using them. Parents gently (and sometimes not so gently) suggest alternative ways we can do our jobs. Fellow teachers share ideas and resources they hope we'll use. Students are constantly asking us questions. Lots of people share their voices, but ultimately, what we do in our classrooms is up to us. We are the deciders, and most of us wouldn't have it any other way.

Autonomy is one of three innate psychological needs all humans require for optimal well-being. Together with competence and relatedness, autonomy comprises self-determination theory, which explains human motivation and personality. People who are trusted to make decisions about their work are happier and more productive employees. Studies looking at autonomy have found that increasing a person's options increases their intrinsic motivation for a task. People crave the ability to choose, and we really like having lots of options. Conversely, we reflexively despise mandates and hate being bossed around.

Like all college students, I was assigned a lot of required reading. I liked reading. Whenever a new Stephen King or John Grisham novel came out, I usually read it within a few weeks. But reading for pleasure ended during my college years, and it was the fault of required reading. I didn't want to read anything I was told to read. And because I wasn't reading what was required, I felt guilty about reading anything else. So I stopped reading altogether. On the other hand, I once wrote a paper about wolves for an English class. Because I was allowed to choose my topic and sources, I didn't mind doing the research. I learned a lot about wolves, some of which I still remember. I even have the paper somewhere in my basement today. It was one of the better ones I wrote, which is consistent with the research on choice.

One of the attractions of the teaching profession is the high amount of freedom educators enjoy relative to other professions. While it is on the decline, 73 percent of teachers in a 2012 survey reported moderate or high levels of autonomy. The highest areas of autonomy included the assigning of homework, the evaluation of students' academic progress, instructional techniques, and student discipline.

Research finds that autonomy is positively associated with teachers' job satisfaction and retention. Teachers who perceive that they have less autonomy are more likely to leave their positions, either by moving from one school to another or leaving the profession altogether. Dr. Richard Ingersoll of the University of Pennsylvania has studied teacher turnover and retention for years. One of the reasons teachers quit, he says, is that they feel micromanaged. They have little say in decisions that ultimately affect their teaching. According to Ingersoll, it's this lack of classroom autonomy that is now the biggest source of frustration for math teachers nationally. "Teachers have been saying for a long time that one size doesn't fit all, all students are different. But they're told to stick to the scripted curriculum, which might work for a weaker teacher but it drives good teachers nuts," he says.

But even though teachers may yearn for and need autonomy to be their best, that control comes at a cost. Teachers who are given a lot of freedom have to make a lot of choices. Like George W. Bush, they have to be deciders, and deciders get tired.

The people who design supermarkets understand this. Nothing in a supermarket is accidental. It's all set up with one goal in mind — to get you to spend more money. When you enter most supermarkets you are met by the sweet aromas emanating from the bakery near the front of the store. The smells of baked bread, cookies, and cake tickle your nose and start your mouth watering. Sale items will soon appear before you, perched on special tables placed right in the center of an aisle, where you can't miss them. Produce will also be near the front of the store because market research shows that when shoppers put healthy food in their carts, they're likely to buy more junk food later on. Junk foods have outstanding profit margins.

Whether you work from front to back or back to front, you'll have to pass every aisle twice because the checkout lanes are at the front of the store.

You'll be tempted to buy the seasonal items, cases of beer, and bags of chips placed in the main thoroughfare each time you exit an aisle. At every turn, you'll be offered options. Scads of options. More options than you can shake a Newman's Own Low-Fat Sesame Ginger bottle of salad dressing at. Twelve varieties of shredded cheese made by four different companies, some discounted, some offered as buy two get a third free. Skim milk, 2 percent milk, whole milk, almond milk, cashew milk, each in different sizes, for different prices, and sporting different brand logos. Nine flavors of pasta sauce, 23 kinds of crackers — some no different except for their shape — and spices, spices, so many spices! Which to choose?

The process continues, over and over, aisle by aisle, product after product. Do you buy the family-sized box of Cheez-Its that's on sale this week, or is it a better deal to buy two smaller boxes? Should you buy the name-brand tortilla chips or will the cheap ones suffice? Do you feel like cutting the ham yourself or do you want it already chopped? You make decision after decision. Most of you do it after a long day of making decisions at work. The peak weekday shopping times are from 4 pm to 7 pm, right when your willpower is at its lowest.

When you're finally done and join the queue in the checkout lane, you're presented with impulse items, so named because you normally wouldn't consider buying them. Tabloids, candy bars, sugary drinks, nail clippers, and gift cards surround you as you wait. Obviously, it works. People buy this stuff, and in fact, these items represent the biggest profit margins in the entire store. There's a good reason they're placed where they are. But *why* do they work? What's going on in your brain that makes you susceptible to buying the *National Enquirer* while you wait to pay for your groceries? Why do you have a sudden urge to grab a Snickers bar when you hardly ever eat candy?

Psychologist Jean Twenge wondered. She had joined Roy Baumeister in his lab for her postdoctoral work and had been reading up on his willpower experiments. She also happened to be planning a wedding. Reading about the depleting effects of willpower, she recalled the exhausting experience of registering for wedding gifts. Making decision after decision had been tiring, and by the end of it, Twenge said she could have been talked into anything.

She sensed a connection. Did making decisions use willpower? It certainly seemed her fatigue matched that of the study participants she'd read about. She decided to test it. Twenge and fellow researchers went out and bought some products they thought would appeal to college kids. They laid the items out on tables and divided the students into two test groups. One group was required to make a series of choices. Researchers asked them to pick between two products with the understanding that their choices would determine which item they would ultimately get to keep. So participants had to choose between items like a pencil or a candle, then a t-shirt or a pen, choice after choice, until the psychologists thought they were sufficiently depleted. The other group made no decisions at all. They were just asked to rate the products on the table and tell how frequently they'd used them in the past six months.

Afterward, all subjects were directed to hold one of their hands in ice water for as long as they could, a common test of willpower because your instinct is to remove it. The students who had made decisions removed their hand much quicker than those who hadn't, a sign that they had less willpower. The same effect turned up in an experiment that required college students to choose their courses for the coming semester, in another that asked students how they would like to be taught in an upcoming class, and in one with mall shoppers who had spent the day deciding which stores to enter and which products to buy.

The more decisions you make, the more willpower you use. The more willpower you use, the less glucose you have in your system. The lower your blood sugar is, the more tired you feel.

In my third grade classroom, we start each morning with a math problem of the day. Students come in, execute the morning routine, and are expected to get right to work. After five or ten minutes, I call on a few students to share their solutions on the board. The total time, from the moment students enter the room, to when we all stand for the Pledge of Allegiance, is about 20 minutes. Here are some decisions I typically make during this time:

- Which math standard the Problem of the Day will introduce or reinforce

- Which specific math problem to put on the board

- How to word the problem so students are exposed to grade-level math vocabulary while also ensuring they are able to understand the problem

- How to react to a student chatting with a friend instead of following the morning procedure

- What to say to a student who forgets to choose a lunch

- How to handle the fact that three students put their backpacks on the ground instead of on the hooks where they're supposed to put them

- What to do about a student who hasn't started her math problem on time

- Whether or not to give hints to those struggling with the problem

- Whether or not to give those hints individually or if the number of struggling students justifies stopping everyone's work to teach something to the whole class

- How much work time to allow

- Whether I should give time for students to share their work with a partner

- What I should do if students don't share work with a partner after being instructed to

- Whether I should call out a student for copying the work of a student seated next to her

- Whether or not to call on a student with her hand up

- Whom to call on to go to the board to share their work

- How to react when some students aren't paying attention to the student sharing his work

- How to respond to a student who has made an error while solving the problem on the board

- Whether I should allow a student requesting to use the restroom to use it at this time

- How to respond to those working at the board so that others would be encouraged to participate in the future

There are two parts to each of those decisions, and indeed, to all decisions. We first weigh the pros and cons. We calculate, evaluate, and deliberate. We acknowledge trade-offs. When deciding which students to call on, teachers quickly consider many factors:

- Do we want someone who has solved the problem correctly?

- Do we want someone who has solved it using a novel strategy that others could learn from?

- Should we choose someone who made a common error so that students' attention can be drawn to it?

- Who haven't we called on in a while?

- Is there a student raising his hand who is normally reluctant to publicly share his work?

- Although we like Malik's method of solving the problem and think it would benefit the class, he's thrusting his arm up and down and grunting. Should we reward such behavior by giving him what he wants or call on someone else? Should we then explain to him why we didn't call on him or trust that he'll figure it out?

Teachers do this kind of deliberating all the time. By itself, it's not that depleting. But then comes the actual decision. The moment to cast the die. The point of no return.

Science has found that it is this act, the committing to a single option, that uses the most willpower.

This may explain why some people put off deciding. What we sometimes refer to as a "fear of commitment" is a reflection of our aversion to loss. Humans feel losses more sharply than they experience gains. Losses stick with us longer. They linger in our conscience. They sting. Consequently, most of us try to avoid them. Anytime we choose — whether it be a spouse, a career, a car, or a new pair of shoes — we are also *not* choosing a lot of other things. We put off marriage, knowing that we're closing the door on dating models (unless we're Tiger Woods, I guess). We buy gift cards, effectively transferring the ultimate, energy-depleting decision to the recipient. We choose two majors, keeping at least one other option open.

In today's world, we are offered far more choices than our ancestors ever had. The pain of closing off options lurks around every corner. If you're a woman who wants a new pair of jeans today, you'll have choices your mother wouldn't even understand. There's low rise, ultra low rise, mid rise, high rise, boyfriend jeans, cigarette jeans, bootcut, flare, wide leg, capri, cropped, cuffed, light washed, ripped, printed, embroidered, and patched. They even have something called shiny jeans now. There are almost as many kinds of jeans as there are uses for shrimp in *Forrest Gump*.

Teachers today also face a dizzying array of choices. Because many of us still enjoy a fair amount of autonomy, we get to decide much of what happens in our classrooms. We choose how we evaluate students. We choose how to organize and decorate our rooms. We make the rules for our classrooms and decide how to enforce them. We make decisions about how much, how often, and what kind of homework to assign. As for instruction, the Internet has grown our options exponentially. While teachers 50 years ago might have had a few choices for how to teach fractions, teachers today can select from hundreds of videos, scores of workbooks, thousands of downloadable worksheets, gobs of online games, and pages of hands-on activities found on Pinterest and other sites. Carnegie Mellon and Temple University researchers found more than 205 *trillion* instructional options available when they considered all the different factors and permutations available from the educational research landscape.

So while teachers like having choices just as much as anybody else, the truth is that the very thing we desire is exhausting us. Choosing is tiring, and there are consequences beyond our flagging energy levels.

Bad Decisions

Imagine you decide to leave your current district at year's end and are fortunate enough to be asked to interview for a job with your dream school. An administrator calls you up and tells you the interviews will take place on a Thursday, and he gives you the option of choosing your slot. Should you interview first, last, or somewhere in the middle?

The right answer is...it depends. Most factors that could affect the interview committee's decision are beyond your control. You can't know the biases each person brings. You won't know whether your interviewers will discuss each candidate in turn or wait until after all interviews have taken place. You don't know what exactly each person is looking for.

But science does suggest that if there are a lot of candidates competing against you and they'll all be interviewed on the same day, then you would benefit from going first. One group of researchers looked at MBA applicants and found that when five similarly qualified candidates were interviewed on the same day, the last one to interview received lower scores than they deserved. The same has been found in many situations where a person is being judged by others whose job it is to make a series of decisions. If you can't be one of the first interviewed, ask to move your appointment to after lunch, so that your interviewers have had a chance to eat and replenish their willpower.

The same effect can be seen in other fields. Doctors are 25 percent more likely to prescribe antibiotics later in the day than in the morning. Judges are more likely to grant parole at the start of the day, after breaks for a morning snack, and after eating lunch, all times when glucose, and therefore willpower, has been restored. Even Major League Baseball managers aren't safe from the effects of decision fatigue. They are statistically more likely to be ejected during the last four innings of a game than they are during the first five. There is also research suggesting that students whose essays get read first receive a fairer grade than those whose are read last.

After a day of making decisions, we don't have the cognitive energy left to make good ones. At worst, we let our heightened emotions and impaired ability to resist temptation get the best of us. We make poor decisions that we later regret. Most of the time, though, we just get lazy. Like doctors who decide to just go ahead and prescribe the antibiotic, we go with the easiest choice. We thoughtlessly accept the recommended option. We focus on a single characteristic, like price, without considering the trade-offs, like quality. When planning a vacation, we overspend because it's easier than thinking. We agree to buy stain protection for our new furniture. We buy the warranty for our new TV. We pay for rust protection on our new car. We keep the criminal in prison instead granting parole because it's easier and less risky. In the classroom, we resort to doing it the way we've always done it. We lecture instead of leading a class discussion. Instead of getting out materials for a hands-on experiment, we pass out textbooks or show a video. We teach it the way we were taught.

It's estimated that teachers make around 1,500 decisions every school day. That works out to four per minute, or one decision every fifteen seconds. Most of them involve energy-depleting trade-offs. When you combine these decisions with all the necessary self-regulation involved with teaching kids, it's a miracle teachers have enough willpower left to safely make the drive home.

Every teacher enjoys being trusted enough by their administration that they are given the freedom to decide what's best for their students. We like being a part of the decision-making process. Being granted autonomy is often seen as a sign of respect, an indication that you're viewed as a professional. Having control over our careers is necessary for our happiness and production. But it's a double-edged sword. The more decisions you make, the more willpower you will use. That will make you tired.

So the next time you're tempted to complain about your district taking away some of your ability to choose, you might remember what choosing does to your brain and your body. Instead of griping, you might decide to see the positive side of things and thank them for cutting back on one of the sources of your exhaustion. With fewer decisions to make, you might even have the energy to swing by the supermarket to pick up ingredients for a healthy dinner. Just be careful. Those checkout lanes are dangerous, and if you've had a long day, you might end up with a bottle of Coke, three Snickers bars, and a tabloid with Tiger Woods's latest girlfriend on the cover.

Get Fired Up!

"Here we are now, entertain us!"

"Smells Like Teen Spirit"
Nirvana

It's easy to forget that Jeb Bush was the early favorite to win the 2016 Republican nomination for the President of the United States. The former governor of Florida, he was the ultimate establishment candidate that could count on the influence and financial contributions of the most powerful forces in the party. He was part of the Bush dynasty, with both his father and older brother serving as Commander-in-Chief. Compared to many of his rivals, Bush seemed eminently qualified. A month into his campaign, Bush's Real Clear Politics polling average was at 17 percent. The next closest candidate, eventual winner Donald Trump, was polling at just over 10 percent. Wall-to-wall press coverage allowed Trump to quickly close that gap and surpass Bush, but it was Trump's incessant verbal assaults on the presumptive nominee that did real damage.

Jeb wasn't alone. Trump repeatedly called Ted Cruz a liar, dubbed Marco Rubio "Little Marco," and insulted Carly Fiorina's looks. But it was his labeling of Bush as "low-energy" that was most effective. Dilbert creator Scott Adams called it a "linguistic kill shot," and it was a wound from which Bush would never recover. The phrase became a measuring stick by which everyone judged Jeb, with potential voters telling him, "You are full of energy. The nation needs to know that," and, "You're more dynamic than I expected." The slight got inside Bush's head. Looking to prove his vitality, he packed his schedule and started shouting his stump speeches, boasting to one crowd that he'd just run three miles. When asked at a debate to select a Secret Service code name, Jeb responded with "Eveready," before telling Trump, "It's very high energy, Donald."

Bush knew how damaging the label was, and he worked tirelessly to shed it. Because of all the things you don't want to be called during a Presidential campaign — stupid, ugly, short, a liar, — none stung as much or hung as heavily around a candidate's neck like being thought of as lacking energy.

Americans believe that to be good at anything, you have to *bring it*. It is embedded deep in our collective conscience — this idea that the only way to achieve is through passion and intensity. Vince Lombardi, one of the most successful coaches in NFL history, famously said, "If you're not fired with enthusiasm, you'll be fired with enthusiasm." Ralph Waldo Emerson believed that, "Nothing great was ever accomplished without enthusiasm." Walter Chrysler echoed, "The real secret to success is enthusiasm." Similar quotes abound from leaders in every walk of life, including education.

You can't spend more than a few minutes at a teaching conference without someone telling you how important it is to be energetic in the classroom. You can't join an education chat on Twitter without hearing the same. Nearly every book about teaching extolls the virtue of teacher intensity as a cure for student boredom, low motivation, and a lack of achievement. Pop culture contributes, as well. Excellent teachers, we are reminded, stand atop desks and shout, "Carpe diem!" (*Dead Poets Society*) They scream, "There are no victims in this classroom!" (*Dangerous Minds*) They're so intense they pick up unmotivated students' desks and slam them on the ground. (*The Ron Clark Story*)

This belief in the power of passion shaped my early years of teaching. I energetically presented a lesson one moment, snapped angrily at a misbehaving student the next, slapped my hand on a desk to drive home a point, and passionately prodded my students to do their best on even mundane tasks. At the end of the school day, I would exhort my students to pick up the trash off the floor. "Come on!, come on! Get all the trash! Pick it all up. I still see five pieces! You have six more seconds to get it all! Six! Five! Four!..." To be any good, I figured, I had to be *intense*. *Fired up!* I needed to be, as Anton Chekhov said, "an actor, an artist, passionately in love" with my work.

We accept the relationship between enthusiasm and success as a given, but does such a relationship actually exist? Are outwardly enthusiastic people more likely to succeed? Are teachers who are intense in the classroom better than those who aren't? In one study of 93 college students, teacher enthusiasm was the most powerful variable of student motivation. A second study of 60 college students found that students who received an enthusiastic lecture reported greater intrinsic motivation for the topic. A 2014 study in Switzerland showed that teacher enthusiasm positively predicted student interest. A 1970 review of the research on teacher enthusiasm found that it was positively associated with student achievement. The research seems clear: Effective teachers are passionate about their jobs, their subjects, and their students.

What is lacking in every study about teacher enthusiasm is an analysis of the costs. Sure, an enthusiastic teacher is better than a dull one, but how long should we expect an enthusiastic teacher to last? Certainly, there are some who can maintain a high amount of energy class after class, day after day. They are born performers, the small percentage for whom teaching really is a calling. They live and breathe this stuff. But for the rest of us, it's literally exhausting.

That's because science has proven that intense emotions, whether good or bad, tire us out.

You can place all emotions into one of four quadrants. On the positive side, you have high-intensity feelings like ecstasy and awe. You also have positive emotions of lower intensity, such as feeling calm or content. High-intensity negative emotions include anguish, anger, and fear. Boredom and melancholy are examples of lower intensity negative emotions.

Low-intensity emotions, whether positive or negative, don't sap our energy much. You can spend the whole day feeling a bit blue or bored without it leading to fatigue. In fact, I am frequently bored during the summer. A month into my summer break, between fun activities like vacations and cookouts, I am sometimes confronted with a prolonged listlessness as I stay home and try not to spend money. I feel adrift, my lack of productivity causing me to question whether I'm wasting precious hours and days of my life. But those thoughts, disquieting as they may sometimes be, don't exhaust me. There is never a summer day that comes close to matching the heavy weight of exhaustion I sometimes feel during the school year.

High-intensity emotions, on the other hand, wear us out. It's easy to understand how negative emotions like frustration, anger, and grief make us tired. Strong feelings like those trigger our stress response. Our bodies respond to those feelings as they respond to any perceived threat. If you spend a large part of your day angry at your students, you'll feel tired at the end of it. Similarly, grief can wipe us out. There's even a phrase — "the lethargy of grief" — to describe the phenomenon. Anguished people often have little energy. Those with depression are sometimes so tired they don't want to get out of bed.

While there are some teachers who rely on the stress response to give them the energy they need to perform, most of us try to avoid high-intensity negative emotions. We don't want to be angry, frustrated, or overcome with anxiety.

What's less understood is that high-intensity *positive* emotions also make teachers tired. These feelings — the kind we're told we need to be effective — involve the same physiological arousal as high-intensity negative emotions. Adrenaline and cortisol course through our bodies, causing a faster pulse and stronger contractions of the heart muscle. Our blood vessels dilate, elevating our blood pressure. Glucose stores are released, giving us the energy to run from danger. Our muscles tense. Our breathing gets faster. Our sweat glands activate. We startle more easily.

Because high-intensity emotions of all kinds activate our body's stress response, the excitement we feel when we teach with great intensity and animation can deplete our systems when sustained over long periods. The chronic stress that results compromises our immunity, our memories, and our attention spans. High-intensity emotions — whether they're negative *or positive* — tax our bodies and leave us exhausted.

High-intensity emotions also stress the brain. It's hard to focus when we're physiologically aroused and overstimulated. We know from brain-imaging research that when we experience intense emotions, the amygdala is activated. We then need to use more effort and emotion-regulation strategies from a different part of our brain to calm ourselves enough to get work done. This emotional regulation itself requires additional effort. And the part of the brain called upon to self-regulate is the same part we need to focus and solve problems.

Research shows that we — especially Westerners, and Americans in particular — thrive on high-intensity positive emotions. Jeanne Tsai of Stanford University found that when you ask Westerners how they would like to feel, they are more likely to name words like *elated* and *euphoric* than low-intensity positive emotions like *relaxed* or *content*. Americans believe that high-intensity emotions lead to success and happiness. East Asian cultures, on the other hand, value low-intensity emotions like serenity and peacefulness.

You can't be a good teacher if you don't like your job. You need passion to excel in the classroom. Excitement is a good thing, and it certainly feels better than anger or anxiety. But high-intensity positive emotions are like chocolate; they're best in small doses. Just as a sugar high will feel great for a while, your energy level will eventually crash. You are bound to feel tired sooner than if you had remained calm.

That's not to say you should never show excitement in the classroom. Teachers should not stand at the front of their rooms and bore their students to tears with droning, monotonous lectures. None of us want to be the economics teacher in *Ferris Bueller's Day Off*. Nor should you lose your enthusiasm for the work or temper your inner passions. Denying your true feelings takes willpower and will tire you out. However, teachers who are sick of feeling exhausted have to attend to and modulate their high-intensity emotions. They must be aware of the effect those emotions have on their bodies, and be intentional about using them for maximum impact.

Not every lesson needs to be presented enthusiastically. If you're concerned students won't find a particular topic motivating, there are ways to inspire outside of relying on the infectious nature of your own passion. Giving students choice, allowing them to work with classmates, incorporating technology, or gamifying the content are some ways teachers make content more appealing without bankrupting their limited supply of energy.

Mundane tasks like organizing supplies, turning in work, or lining up to leave the classroom do not require impassioned coaxing. Students will probably work better if you aren't flitting around the room, loudly encouraging them to do their best. If you're fired up all day long, zipping back and forth between high-intensity emotions, you're going to risk transferring that frenetic energy to your students. A more excitable class will present you with more behavior problems, which will make your job even more exhausting. You'll be more emotional, use more willpower to suppress your natural reactions to those emotions, and in the long run, you'll be a less effective teacher. Energy and passion are great things, and you should possess them in large quantities, but you shouldn't use them all day. Your excitement, combined with your moments of anger, frustration, and even elation, will tire you out.

In part two of this book, I'll explain why teachers should aim for a feeling of inner calm for large chunks of their day. I'll argue that the expectation we have for ourselves and other teachers to be constantly enthusiastic is counterproductive in the short-term and ultimately damaging to the education system in the long-run. And I'll explain how being calm will not only conserve your energy, but will make your classroom a better learning environment for your students.

It's All In Your Head

"The belief in a thing makes it happen."

Frank Lloyd Wright

31-year-old Kyle Maynard has already lived an extraordinary life. Despite having arms that end at the elbows and legs that stop at the knees, Kyle has been inducted into the wrestling Hall of Fame, won an ESPN Espy Award for Best Athlete with a Disability, was the GNC World's Strongest Teen of 2004, and became the first quadruple amputee to climb Mount Kilimanjaro without assistance, scaling all 19,340 feet in just ten days. He's also a business owner, motivational speaker, and a *New York Times* bestselling author.

Kyle loved sports as a child and grew up playing football. In middle school, he played nose tackle, where his limbless body gave him leverage against offensive linemen who could never get as low as him. As running backs crashed through the line, Kyle would fling his head and shoulders at their legs, bringing them to the ground. His dad convinced him that wrestling would improve his tackling, so Kyle took that sport up, too. For the first year and a half, he lost every match.

Kyle begged his parents to let him quit. But his father told him that when he first started wrestling he hadn't won any matches either. Hardly anybody did their first year. But if Kyle tried again in seventh grade, his dad assured him, he was bound to win because he'd eventually wrestle a beginner. It was nonsense, but Kyle bought it, and he now calls his decision to return to the mat the best of his life. That seventh grade year, after 35 straight losses, Kyle finally won. He said:

"It really had nothing to do with the physical side of things, but for a long time I bought into the belief of other people telling me that I'd never win a match, so I didn't."

Kyle had discovered his secret to success: an unwavering faith in himself and his ability to do anything. Once Kyle Maynard understood the potency of self-belief, he became unstoppable.

Our thoughts are amazingly powerful. Science has found that if you believe a task is going to be difficult, it will be. If you expect a meeting to drain your energy, it will. People who feel old die younger. If the fear of failure overwhelms you, it's likely to result in bad decisions that lead to failure. We tend to get what we expect. When it comes to how tired you feel, your thoughts have a greater impact than you might think.

Almost every distance runner talks of hitting a wall. In 2012 Spanish researchers wanted to know what went through runners' minds as they neared exhaustion, and they found exactly what you'd expect: The harder runners work and the longer they run, the more negative their thoughts become. No surprise there.

But then a group of British and Dutch researchers asked an interesting question. They wondered if everybody had it backward. Did the discomfort of physical fatigue cause the runners to think negatively, like everyone assumed, or did the runners' negative thoughts make them more physically tired and sore? It was a chicken and egg question.

The researchers found 24 healthy adults and had each complete a grueling ride on a stationary bike until they were exhausted. Then they sent them home for two weeks. During that time, half of the subjects were trained in positive self-talk, a technique many sports psychologists and coaches teach athletes to combat negative thinking that can lead to poor performance. The other twelve subjects were left alone. Then the researchers called them all back to hop on the bikes again.

On average, those who received positive self-talk training performed more than 17 percent better on their second ride than they had on their first. There was no improvement among members of the control group. The cause of the improvement among the self-talk subjects was therefore entirely mental. The training in positive self-talk reduced perceptions of fatigue during the exercise test, which enabled them to pedal longer before reaching intolerable levels of exertion.

The study indicates that negative thoughts during strenuous exercise are not the *result* of fatigue. Negative thoughts are the *cause* of fatigue.

Before the mid-1970's no human had ever lifted 500 pounds overhead. The great Russian weightlifter Vasily Alexeyev held the world record, but could not break the 500-pound barrier. During one competition, his trainers told him that he would be lifting a weight he had lifted before — 499.9 pounds. After a successful lift, he discovered that his trainers had lied. He had actually lifted 500.5 pounds — a new world record.

By telling him to do something he already knew he could do, Alexseyev's trainers had removed the mental boundary he had set, and once the 500-pound barrier was broken, Alexseyev and other weightlifters were soon lifting considerably more than that. Vasily Alexeyev himself went on to lift more than 560 pounds overhead. He told *Sports Illustrated*, "For some performers, there is a psychological problem. As the weight is greater, the more the mind makes the weight seem to be."

More often than not, the driving force behind our exhaustion isn't the hours we work, the challenges we face in the classroom, or the lack of support from administration. It is our thoughts. We make the weights heavier than they are. And one of the most common types of negative thinking is worry.

Teachers worry for lots of reasons:

- Students aren't learning
- A lesson is bombing
- We have a sub tomorrow
- A parent is angry
- The principal is coming to observe our teaching
- The copy machine is down and what are we going to do now?
- A colleague is mad at us
- We showed a movie and a character said a bad word and now the kids might go home and tell mom and dad and they'll call the principal and we never even filled out the stupid form we're supposed to fill out for the movie and...

When we worry, we imagine and anticipate negative events. All worries are, at their cores, expressions of fear. When we worry about a job interview, we fear we're going to get stumped by a question, look like a fool, and have to live in our parents' basement. When we worry about an upcoming observation, we fear our lesson will fall flat, our students will misbehave, and our evaluation will be so bad we'll get fired and have to live in our parents' basement.

Because we treat worry as a threat, our bodies respond the same way they react to physical danger.

To help us cope with the demands we are about to ask our bodies to perform, our brains prime us for action. We go into survival mode.

But most of the things teachers worry about cannot be dealt with by fighting or running away. A visit from the principal, an angry email from a parent, an argument with a colleague, or unrealistic expectations cannot be resolved physically (at least not legally), so our bodies remain in a state of anxiety, poised for action.

The resulting tension can cause headaches, back pain, weak legs, and trembling. At the same time, our digestive system slows down as energy is redirected to deal with the demands the stress response has placed on our bodies. As a result, our immune response is weakened, making us more susceptible to colds or more serious illnesses. With excessive worry, our immune systems have little time to recover, so we become even more tired and lethargic.

Worrying also affects our brains. It disturbs our peace of mind, making it harder to concentrate on anything other than our fears. This can make it difficult to fall asleep at night. A lack of sleep means you won't be replenishing all of the energy you used today, making tomorrow even more of a challenge and exacerbating the likelihood of chronic fatigue. Excessive worry can even lead to depression.

There are four ways worrying makes you tired:

Disturbed Sleep

Worrying can prevent you from falling asleep at night. You'll be unable to turn off your brain as you lie there turning over scenarios in your mind. Once you do nod off, your fears will linger subconsciously and may wake you earlier than you wanted. A lack of sleep undermines performance. For a teacher, a good night's rest is essential. To be our best, we must be engaged and observant. One study concluded that foregoing sleep for 17-19 hours impairs the body as much as a blood-alcohol level of 0.05. No teacher would consider showing up to class after slamming a couple of drinks, but when worrying deprives you of sleep, that's basically what you're doing. 48 percent of Americans report losing sleep due to stress. Given the elevated stress levels for teachers, it's likely that more than half of American teachers are experiencing the negative effects of sleep deprivation in their classrooms.

Adrenaline Crashes

When you worry your body incorrectly assumes you're in danger and releases adrenaline, which acts as a stimulant to help you fight or flee that danger. As with all stimulants, when this adrenaline rush ends, you'll experience a crash. This can cause sudden and severe fatigue. If you worry constantly, then your body will be in a permanent cycle of adrenaline rushes and crashes, leading to feelings of total exhaustion.

Adrenal Fatigue

If you're anxious all the time, your adrenal glands will constantly release adrenaline and eventually become exhausted. It's called adrenal fatigue. The result is your adrenal glands shut down and can no longer release adrenaline in big enough quantities to get you through the day. In this state, physical, emotional, and psychological stress of any kind will immediately exhaust you.

Mental Fatigue

If you're constantly experiencing worries, stress, and negative thoughts, you will cope by either denying you have them or repressing them so as to appear unaffected around others. Both repression and denial take a huge amount of mental energy, and mental energy eventually runs out just like physical energy. Teachers with negative thoughts about their jobs often try to hide those emotions, at least in front of their students. It takes willpower to "put on a happy face," and using willpower, as you already know, is tiring.

Carol Dweck is best known among teachers as the pioneering psychologist behind mindsets. She identified a fixed mindset as belonging to those who believe they're essentially born with a set amount of intelligence and talent. Conversely, those with a growth mindset believe they can improve with practice. Dweck performed some experiments with children demonstrating the effects of teaching students a growth mindset, and her findings have been used by teachers all over the world to motivate students to try their best to improve.

Less well-known is Dweck's investigations into the effects of mindset on willpower. She discovered something that, in light of everything you've read so far, shouldn't surprise you.

If you believe using willpower is depleting, then it will be more depleting.

In other words, Dweck's research shows that it really is mind over matter. You can talk yourself into believing you have plenty of willpower left. You can talk yourself into believing stress is good for you. You can talk yourself into believing you're not tired. So if you want to know why you're tired all the time, the simplest answer is because you think you are.

PART TWO:

WHAT TO DO ABOUT IT

Work Less

"You don't have to go home, but you can't stay here."

"Closing Time"
Semisonic

Henry Ford is often portrayed as a champion of the working man for doubling his employees' hourly pay, cutting their hours to 40 per week, and giving them weekends off. But Ford wasn't acting out of a sense of altruism, and he didn't give a hoot about bolstering America's middle class. He was just trying to sell more cars.

By 1913, Ford had developed all of the basic techniques of the assembly line. It was a technological marvel that cut the time it took to build a car from more than 12 hours to just 90 minutes. Production jumped from 70,000 cars in 1912 to 170,000 in the year the assembly line was introduced. There was only one thing preventing even greater efficiency: Ford's workers.

Ford's innovations were hard on employees, and turnover was extremely high. In 1913, Ford hired more than 52,000 men to staff a workforce of just 14,000. Sometimes, workers simply didn't show up.

Many walked off the job to go work somewhere else. Delays in production were frequent, and hiring new people was expensive and time-consuming. New workers needed to be trained, and once on the job, they were slower than the experienced men they'd replaced. The problem kept Ford from selling cars at the low price he wanted. Drastic measures were needed.

Ford had kept meticulous records, and by 1914, backed by 12 years of in-house research on productivity, he boldly introduced the five-dollar day and reduced shifts from nine hours to eight. He also lopped a day off the work week, freeing up both Saturday and Sunday for his employees.

The National Association of Manufacturers criticized him harshly. Wall Street wasn't happy. But Henry Ford was. Turnover plunged. The cost per vehicle plummeted. Productivity surged. Ford Motor Company doubled its profits in less than two years. Sales in 1914 reached 308,162, and 501,462 in 1915. By 1920, production exceeded one million cars a year. Henry Ford would call the reforms the best cost-cutting moves he ever made. As they watched his sales skyrocket, Ford's competitors and those in other industries followed suit. Soon, many of the country's workers were working fewer hours, often with better pay. The nation had learned an important lesson:

When it comes to the number of hours you work, less is more.

It's a lesson we've forgotten in education. Legislators add days to the school calendar. Administrators ladle on more work and rarely take anything off teachers' plates. Parents expect teachers to stay after school to meet with them or tutor their kids. And many teachers have bought into the dangerous assumption that overwork is a necessary precondition for success in the classroom.

You can always do more. You can always come in earlier and stay later. There's enough work to fill a 60-hour or even an 80-hour work week. But just because others are doing it, and just because administration has piled your responsibilities so high it feels as if you'll never dig out from under them, doesn't mean you should. As Henry Ford learned, working more does not guarantee better results. In fact, it's the opposite.

Hundreds of studies conducted in the decades following Ford's reforms proved him right. The benefits of the 40-hour week were once so accepted by corporate America that in 1962 the Chamber of Commerce published a pamphlet highlighting the productivity gains of reduced hours. The studies concluded that industrial workers can give eight productive hours per day. On average, you'll get no more out of a factory worker logging a 10-hour day than you will out of one clocking out after eight. When it comes to knowledge workers like teachers, the research shows that we're only capable of six productive hours a day. So teachers may stay longer if their principals ask them to, but once the kids are gone, they're not going to do anyone much good.

While it's important to limit how much time you spend at work, it's not merely the number of hours that are exhausting you. That common misconception treats all hours the same, but you know from personal experience that's not true. Twelve hours spent doing stress-free, enjoyable activities do not wear you out like twelve hours of labor-intensive work. A day at the beach is not the same as a day digging ditches. Seven hours with a well-behaved class are less exhausting than seven hours with a challenging one. It's not the number of hours you work, it's the nature of those hours.

Most of those hours, if you're a teacher, are stressful and exhausting. You must exercise willpower at all times. You make hundreds of decisions. You emotions volley from excitement to anger to fear to exasperation. You worry about your students, your performance, and how others perceive you. You engage in negative self-talk because no matter how much you do and how effective you are, there's always more to be done and a handful of students for whom your methods failed.

The longer you're under stress, the more tired you will feel. Ending your day shortly after students leave is the simplest way to conserve willpower, make fewer decisions, worry less, and end work stress so that you have enough energy to live your life. In short, if you're tired of being tired, work less.

Go Home

When you get full and your stomach starts to hurt, you stop eating. When you can no longer keep your eyes open, you go to bed. When you're on the treadmill and out of breath, you stop running until you've recovered. When our bodies tell us to knock it off, most of us listen. But when it's our brains that are tired, many of us continue plowing ahead, convinced we can will ourselves to perform.

A lot of teachers stay after school because they have work to do, but they've chosen the worst possible time to get it done. Willpower is what you need to make yourself check papers, read essays, plan lessons, and respond tactfully to emails. A lack of willpower means your after-school efforts are going to be inefficient. You'll be more easily distracted, more tempted to surf the web or gossip with colleagues, and more likely to head to the lounge to eat whatever you can find because your body needs fuel.

You will also be fighting against Parkinson's Law. It states that work will expand to fill the available time. I wrote and published my first two books, *The Teacher's Guide to Weight Loss* and *Happy Teacher* in two months each. I was able to do that because that's how long I gave myself to complete them. I allowed myself five months to complete this book, and I'll give you one guess how long it's taken me. This is Parkinson's Law at work, and it will strike you as you sit at your desk after school. Instead of working until you complete a certain amount of work — a task that could take hours — give yourself 30 minutes. You'll be more focused, your work will be of better quality, and you'll cut out distractions and unnecessary extras.

Give yourself less time, and you'll get more done.

Remember, more work doesn't equal more output. In one study, managers couldn't tell the difference between employees who worked 80-hour weeks and those who just pretended to (which somehow sounds worse). Numerous studies have shown that overwork leads to stress that causes sleep deprivation, depression, heart disease, memory loss, and greater alcoholic intake. Researchers have also found that working too much impairs your abilities to communicate, make judgments, read others' nonverbal language, and regulate your emotions.

If you're used to staying two hours after school, start going home earlier and instead come in one hour before schools starts. It's a simple formula:

Time before school is worth twice as much as time after school.

Take advantage of the morning morality effect. You'll give in to fewer temptations because you'll have a full complement of willpower. You'll be more focused on your to-do list. Colleagues who happen to also be at school early will likewise be more focused. They'll be less likely to distract you with conversation. So go home. Get rest. Exercise. Live your life. And come to school the next day refreshed and ready to start again.

Say No

Teachers who want to go home and have more energy must first stop volunteering to further exhaust themselves. They have to start saying no.

Teachers try to do it all, and not only does this approach guarantee we do few things exceptionally well, but we exhaust ourselves in the process of achieving such predictable mediocrity. Teachers who have a hard time saying no must first recognize that every choice they make has trade-offs. Anytime you say yes to one thing, you're saying no to others. By agreeing to stay after school to organize the science kits, you're saying no to things like planning better lessons, checking papers, eating dinner with your family, exercising, and getting a full night's rest.

In his book, *Essentialism*, Greg McKeown suggests that one way to say no more often is to ask yourself, *What problem do I want?* He explains:

"The more we think about what we are giving up when we say yes to someone, the easier it is to say no. If we have no clear sense of the opportunity cost — in other words, the value of what we are giving up — then it is especially easy to fall into the trap of telling ourselves we can get it all done."

So, would you rather disappoint your colleagues by not attending the after-school culture-building get-together? Or would you rather upset your spouse by coming home late from work again? Which problem do you want? When teachers begin prioritizing and only doing those things that further their professional and personal goals, saying no becomes easier.

Author Tim Ferriss takes this kind of thinking to the extreme. When deciding whether or not to take on new projects, his decision-making model is, "If it's not a hell yeah, then it's a no." Such a high standard is a good way to ensure you're only doing those things you care most about.

Education is notorious for asking teachers to do more, and teachers, in their earnestness to be the best they can, try to do it all. The next time an administrator asks you to do something new, remind her that trade-offs always exist by saying, "I am happy to do that. What should I give less priority to in order to do it well?"

If you start to feel guilty about cutting back, remind yourself that saying no isn't selfish. Saying no frees you up to do things that matter most. It focuses you and makes you more effective at the important things you choose to do.

Stop Creating

Do you make your own clothes? Do you grow most of your own food? Did you build the car your drive? Not me. Those things are time-consuming, I don't know how to do any of them, and I can go somewhere and buy all of them for less than I can make them (especially when you factor in the costs of inevitable mistakes).

Have you ever designed your own science unit? Do you make your own writing rubrics? Write your own tests? Ever create your own worksheets? Why?

Once upon a time, people did have to make their own clothes and grow their own food. And once upon a time, teachers did have to create their own instructional materials. They don't have to anymore. Times change. And one of the biggest changes to education in the last twenty years was the adoption of the Common Core State Standards (CCSS) by many states.

It's safe to say that the Common Core wouldn't exist without Bill Gates's money and influence. Gates's involvement in the Core can be traced back to a summer meeting in 2008, described by Lindsey Layton in a 2014 article for the Washington Post:

"Gene Wilhoit, director of a national group of state school chiefs, and David Coleman, an emerging evangelist for the standards movement, spent hours in Bill Gates's sleek headquarters near Seattle, trying to persuade him and his wife, Melinda, to turn their idea into reality.

Coleman and Wilhoit told the Gateses that academic standards varied so wildly between states that high school diplomas had lost all meaning, that as many as 40 percent of college freshmen needed remedial classes, and that U.S. students were falling behind their foreign competitors.

The pair also argued that a fragmented education system stifled innovation because textbook publishers and software developers were catering to a large number of small markets instead of exploring breakthrough products. That seemed to resonate with the man who led the creation of the world's dominant computer operating system."

Gates later participated in an interview with the American Enterprise Institute, and spoke about his efforts to promote the Common Core:

"If [states] have two [sets of standards] they're comparing, they ought to probably pick something in common because, to some degree, this is an area where, if you do have commonality, it's like an electrical plug, you get more free market competition. Scale is good for free market competition."

Scale is also good for teachers looking to spend less time making stuff.

Since nearly every state, even those that have nominally rejected the CCSS, has essentially the same learning expectations, there is now a mountain of available resources that align with the content educators are required to teach. Publishers have benefitted from the standards (as have sellers on Teachers Pay Teachers) because they can now sell to an entire nation of educators, not just those in their own states. Almost all of the online sites I use with my students did not exist before the Common Core State Standards.

No matter what you think of the Common Core or the motives of Bill and Melinda Gates and corporate publishers, every teacher should take advantage of the opportunity the standards provide to create less. There is almost never a good reason to spend your most precious resource making content anymore. Somebody somewhere has already invested the time and mental capital to do so. Take advantage of it, and spend your energies elsewhere.

Stop Taking Student Work Home

There are lots of strategies you can use to reduce the amount of student work you take home, thereby cutting the number of hours your pour into the job. I'll be writing about these in an upcoming book, but to summarize, you can try the following:

Use Class Time To Check Student Work

Teachers feel guilty when they're not directly involved with their students. They think they shouldn't check papers, complete administrative tasks, or answer parent emails when students are in the room. But all of those things are part of the job. They're expected of you. You shouldn't put on a Bill Nye video so you can hop on Facebook, but if your students are working on a test, and all you're going to be doing is walking around making sure their eyes are on their own papers, stop and take care of some of your other responsibilities.

I once had a colleague who was "caught" checking papers at her desk by her principal. She'd check some work and then call students up to discuss it. The principal, unimpressed by her use of time, made some snide remark, to which she rightly responded, "I'm giving immediate feedback. It's best practice!"

Instead of assigning 20 math problems, watching students work, then taking home a stack of papers to correct, assign five, have students show them to you when they finish in class, circle the ones they miss right in front of them, and have them fix the problems right there. It's more effective feedback for students, and it helps free up your nights. Assessment expert Jan Chappuis says, "Effective feedback occurs during the learning, while there is still time to act on it." This can only happen when students are present.

Leverage Technology

If you're fortunate enough to work in a school with Chromebooks, laptops, or tablets, you have the opportunity to significantly reduce the amount of work you take home. In the past, all student work had to be checked by the teacher. Now, technology can take over this time-consuming task and quickly provide you with information about your students that used to take hours. The big publishers provide online components with their programs that include ways to assess students. Students who take their reading or math tests on a computer receive immediate feedback on their performance. You quickly learn their strengths and weaknesses. Using quiz-making software, teachers can create their own quick assessments (or better yet, find some created by others, such as those on Kahoot or Quizizz).

Technology can also help with the time-consuming task of grading student writing. I've never found writing grades particularly helpful to students, but feedback is a must. Even professional writers seek out and benefit from feedback. Technology allows teachers to provide feedback at the very moment when it can be used best — when students are working on their drafts. By having students share their writing with you, you can watch them type in real-time and leave comments right on their screens. Many of my writing conferences are now digital conferences, where I sit with seven tabs of student documents open on my laptop. Switching between them, I highlight and leave comments, pointing out things students are doing well and areas where they can improve. The next day, I provide feedback to another seven students. In this manner, I can see everyone's writing within a week. By the time I have to "grade" their papers, I have already provided a lot of support and the students' writing is better because of it.

Teachers also sometimes forget that they aren't the only ones from whom students can learn. When students finish a draft, I have them share it with three other students and require those students to provide feedback on the work. They often parrot the kinds of comments I make, which reinforces the messages I send students about good writing.

Don't Grade Everything

I'm willing to bet there's nothing in your contract that says you have to grade every assignment you give students. And yet I know many teachers who do just that. When you have a pile of papers to grade, ask yourself the following questions:

- Does this paper need to be graded? Will students benefit from a grade? Will a grade lead to more learning? Will a grade guide my instruction or interventions?

- Am I grading this paper for students, parents, or for some other reason?

- Will grading this paper give me information that I can use?

- If I do have to grade it, do I need to grade everything, or will grading only some of it suffice?

You may decide that a paper does not need to be graded. Math practice pages are just that, practice. While you might benefit from seeing how students are doing on the practiced math skill, it's unnecessary to grade every single problem to determine who needs reteaching. A quick scan will usually reveal that information.

Even if you feel you owe it to your students to provide feedback on everything you assign, you can focus your feedback on just one area or just a handful of problems. In writing, don't score six different traits for every submitted piece, grade one piece for one trait and other pieces for other traits.

Another strategy is to collect all student homework, but only grade some of it. Introduce the concept of sampling to your students and explain that not every assignment will be graded, but some will. To ensure accountability, make sure they understand that those that are scored will count toward their final grade.

Stop Assigning Things

If you decide there are some assignments you're not going to grade, then the next question you should ask is whether or not students need to do such assignments in the first place. I used to assign my students math worksheets at the end of each week. I never graded them. I justified this by telling myself that the homework was simply practice. By doing it, students would gain fluency. But I noticed that I couldn't really tell the difference between those students who were completing the homework and those who weren't. I also had to admit that some students who never turned in homework did just fine on the summative tests. And, I had to admit that there were other students who did every page of homework, but still did poorly on the tests. It seemed that homework wasn't doing much good at all. So I effectively got rid of it. To appease parents who believe in its value, I made it optional. If parents wanted it, they had to let me know, otherwise I didn't send any home. About half of my students receive homework this year, and only half of those turn it in. I've noticed no difference in test scores.

Change Your Perspective

On the last school day of each year, my district recognizes retiring teachers at an ice cream social. The entire faculty attends. The principals of the retiring teachers stand up and tell some bad jokes, then they say some nice things about the teachers.

One year, one of the principals started her speech by talking about how dedicated Judy was. "Anyone who knows Judy knows that she's the first one here and the last one to leave every day, even after all these years," she said. We were supposed to be impressed. I wasn't.

There are two types of workaholics, and neither of them deserve our admiration. The first type of workaholic is the kind of person who has great passion for and is highly skilled at his job. He gets up in the morning and can't wait to get started. He works all hours of the night because it's a thrill. He gets a buzz off it. Rather than burning him out, the work invigorates him. It's in his blood. When we think of people like this, we often can't help but think of them in any way other than their association with their life's passion. Think of Steve Jobs and you think of Apple. Think of Mark Zuckerberg and you think of Facebook.

These people are often looked up to, but should we really admire those who obsessively spend untold hours doing the very things that give them extreme pleasure?

We don't admire other people for excessively doing that which they love. There will be no biopics about a 35-year-old man who spends most of his time playing video games in his parents' basement. We don't hold degenerate gamblers in high esteem. No one grows up aspiring to a lifetime of debt because they love to shop.

There's a name we give to people who can't stop doing things they love to the detriment of other areas of their lives. We call them addicts. How is being addicted to one's work fundamentally different from being addicted to heroin, pornography, or gambling? Why should anyone admire a workaholic who does nothing but dedicate countless hours to something he really *really* gets off on? The only difference between workaholics and addicts is that society values the workaholics' addiction more than the addicts'. It shouldn't.

The second type of workaholic are those who don't love their jobs, but squander the best hours of their lives at them anyway. They miss out on large parts of their kids' childhoods, strain relationships with those who love them, and make themselves miserable for the sake of pride, a misguided sense of dedication, guilt, or the almighty dollar. If you've seen *The Wolf of Wall Street*, then you're familiar with an extreme example.

There is nothing to revere about someone whose insatiable appetite for approval and recognition destroys so many aspects of the rest of their lives. Workaholics like these wouldn't exist if society did not reward them with the very thing they so desperately want, its admiration.

Some teachers genuinely love the job. They are passionate and skilled. For them, teaching is not really work. The long days don't burn them out. They get physically tired, but not mentally or spiritually drained. They're in flow when teaching. These teachers are rare. Many of them are excellent. But we should stop holding them up as a standard to which all teachers should aspire. You can't instill passion where it doesn't exist, and if the only people we're willing to put at the heads of classrooms are those who live and breathe all things teaching, then class sizes are about to skyrocket. The world needs a *lot* of teachers. The U.S. alone has more than three million of them. You're not going to find that many teaching addicts, and thank goodness for that.

The rest of the workaholic teachers aren't likely to make it very long. They are exhausted. Many are on the verge of burning out. They're under the false impression that to be any good, they must put in long hours. They've lost any semblance of a work-life balance. They're giving up so much because they feel external pressure to do so. They're leaving the profession, sharing their stories, and those stories are keeping young people from even considering a career in the classroom.

We've done that to them. When we as a society admire workaholic teachers, we send the message that all teachers must break their backs to be valued. It's a dangerous message, and the high levels of stress, burnout, and attrition we have today are the result.

Win with Willpower

"It does not do to leave a live dragon out of your calculations, if you live near him."

J.R.R. Tolkien
The Hobbit

Micah Solomon was already frustrated, and knowing what he was about to endure did nothing to lift his spirits. A dusting of snow had left his January flight grounded for a couple of hours in Philadelphia, which had made him late for his connecting flight out of Denver. Deplaning at Denver International, Solomon was already dreading the next few hours. He would either need to stand in the kind of endless, soul-sucking line that makes it feel as though the world is conspiring against you to satisfy its own dark pleasures, all for the privilege to plead his case for a rebooking to an unsympathetic airline employee, or he'd need to call an 800 number, where he'd be put on hold and forced to listen to a robotic recording on repeat, possibly taking turns with some unpleasant noise masquerading as music, for who knew how long. As this future unfolded depressingly through his mind, he was met by a smiling gate agent from Southwest Airlines.

"What's your name?" she asked.

Solomon told her. Within seconds, he was handed a ticket with his name on it for the very next available flight to his destination. The agent had retrieved it from a bundle of already rebooked tickets she was holding.

As Solomon explained in an article for *Forbes*:

"The reason Southwest was able to pull this off wasn't that an empathetic gate agent spontaneously decided to print out these boarding passes. It happened because empathetic people working at Southwest realized that 99+% of the people on the late-arriving plane would want to be rebooked on the next flight out of there. And they therefore designed the process to make this happen, without a single passenger even needing to make a request."

Solomon's story is a good example of exemplary customer service. But it's also a model for how anticipation and systemic improvements can solve problems before they begin. It's this kind of preventive action that's the key to using less willpower.

Even if you cut your hours and stop donating labor, and even if you start saying no and leaving school shortly after your students, you will likely still be leaving the building tired if you spend all day using willpower. It's important to remember that willpower is like a muscle: It can be strengthened with use, but it can also be overworked, leaving you unable to rely on it without recovery time. If you've taught for even a few years, you likely have a large amount of willpower. That's a good thing, because you use a lot of it.

Each time you use willpower, you deplete your supply of it, making it less likely you will have any left at the end of the day and also seriously taxing your body. If you want more energy at the end of the day, you need ways to conserve willpower. Follow Southwest's lead and prepare ahead of time for predictable challenges. To start, avoid placing yourself in situations where you know you'll need to rely on willpower. Don't be like John Edwards.

In 2006, Edwards was contemplating throwing his hat into the ring for the 2008 Presidential election. At the same time, his wife's breast cancer had returned. Having an extramarital affair go public in the middle of a national campaign while your wife underwent treatment for an incurable form of cancer would be a guaranteed way to drive a spike through any and all political aspirations. It would also make you a giant cad.

One place you should not be if you're trying to stay faithful to your cancer-stricken wife is in a hotel bar after a long day with said wife nowhere around. But that's where Edwards found himself on a cold February night. And if you're not interested in committing adultery, you don't stroll over to the attractive blonde who's gaping at you from across the room. But

Edwards did. And when that woman says, "You are so hot," you don't invite her up to your room. I don't know if Edwards was hoping to meet a woman other than his wife that night, but he did nothing to avoid what should have been a perfectly predictable temptation.

Most of the time, we can anticipate situations that will require willpower. I know that certain students are going to push my buttons and tempt me to respond in emotional and possibly unprofessional ways. I know that if I don't work on my classroom newsletter early in the week I'll have to force myself to do it Thursday night, when I really won't want to, or Friday morning, when I have a ton of other things to do. I know that when I get on the highway at five p.m., I am going to get frustrated with traffic and have to use willpower to remain patient at the wheel.

Had John Edwards wanted to remain faithful to his wife, he would have avoided placing himself in a position where he was likely to be tempted at a time when his willpower was depleted. He would have gone directly to his room instead of lounging at the lobby bar.

As a teacher, you usually know where the landmines are buried. Plan ahead to avoid them. I once had a student who could not handle the transition from recess back to the classroom. Unable to settle down, he'd cause problems in the line. Those problems would carry over into the room. Eventually, we worked out a plan where he would go from the playground to the library and help reshelve books for five minutes before returning to class. Another year, I had a student who kept bringing Pokémon cards to school and playing with them when he should have been working. I would get annoyed and take the cards. At first, I'd give them back at day's end. Then I made a rule that a parent had to come retrieve them. When this student's parent did just that and the student continued to bring the cards, I had to change the rule. Now he could only get them back on the last day of school. Finally, he stopped bringing the cards. I learned an important lesson. At the start of every year since then, I tell parents and students that any toy I take won't be returned until the end of the year. I've had very few toys in my room since then.

Sometimes, we can't avoid temptations and distractions. While we may know that certain students in our rooms are going to put our willpower to the test, there's nothing we can do to avoid it. We can, however, anticipate potential interactions and establish if/then plans to deal with them in ways that limit the need for willpower. That is exactly what Starbucks did when they introduced their LATTE training system to improve customer service.

As Charles Duhigg tells it in his book, *The Power of Habit*, Starbucks was struggling back in 2008 when former CEO Howard Schultz was asked to return to his leadership role. Schultz determined that executives had neglected customer service to focus on growth. An internal study had found that most customer service failures happened during moments of high stress, such as busy periods or when dealing with angry customers. So Starbucks gave their baristas very detailed systems to use when dealing with these situations, especially for when their willpower was low. Baristas were instructed to:

L — Listen to the customer

A — Acknowledge their complaint

T — Take action by solving the problem

T — Thank the customer

E — Explain why the problem occurred

They were trained to deal with customers who were in a hurry differently than customers who needed more personal attention. Like all good teachers, managers drilled employees on various scenarios until they knew how to handle any situation.

As a teacher, you can implement your own if/then plans for dealing with stressful situations. Simply prepare yourself ahead of time for how you will handle a defiant student, an angry parent, or a critical administrator. Your classroom management plan should serve your needs in the classroom. Establish clear rules and consistent consequences and let them do the heavy lifting. For special circumstances, decide ahead of time how you'll react to disrespect, emotional outbursts, and other rare but stressful situations. Write down your if/then plans and visualize yourself using them. Examples might include:

- If a student loses control and starts knocking over desks, I will remain calm, have all other students line up and exit the room, and use my cell phone to notify the office.

- If a parent gets in my face, I will calmly say, "I understand that you're upset. I'll be happy to speak with you when I have the time to give you my full attention."

- If the principal criticizes my performance, I will stay calm and say, "You've given me a lot to think about. I appreciate the feedback."

What you're really doing is building new habits so you don't have to use willpower when the stressful moment arrives. Researchers have found that those with the most self-control spend *less* time resisting temptations than others. Dutch researchers concluded that people with good self-control primarily use it to develop good habits at work and school, removing the need to use it to avoid desires. People with high self-control report less stress in their lives not because they use willpower to resist temptations, but to avoid them in the first place.

Think of your pantry. You likely have a mix of healthy snacks and junk food. You might have a bag of apples not too far from a bag of Cheetos. When you're hungry after work and reach for a snack, you'll need to call on willpower that may no longer be available to choose an apple over the Cheetos. But the smarter move would be to not buy the Cheetos in the first place. No willpower necessary. It's the apples or nothing.

People who use willpower preemptively establish good habits like making exercise a part of their morning routine so they don't need to count on willpower to force themselves to go to the gym at night. They start projects early so they don't need to force themselves to pull all-nighters the day before a due date. They pay attention in class so they don't need to will themselves to cram the night before a test. They don't apply for credit cards instead of relying on willpower to keep themselves from buying things they don't need and can't afford.

The lesson for teachers who want to use less self-control and have less stress in their lives is clear:

Use willpower to build habits that will make it less likely you'll need to use willpower.

Instead of willing yourself to read through all your student journals over the weekend, set up a system where five students turn in their journals each day and you always read them at the same time and place. In time it will become a habit that will require no willpower from you. Instead of relying on willpower to read and reply to emails, start a new habit of always reading and replying while you eat lunch, or in the fifteen minutes after school, or whenever is most convenient for you. The key is to do it every day so it becomes a habit and saves you from forcing yourself to do it.

No matter what new habits you create and how well you proactively use willpower to avoid using it when you're stressed and in a "hot" state, you will still need considerable amounts of willpower during your school day. It's just the nature of the job. Fortunately, science has proven that you can increase your willpower in very simple ways so that you'll still have some left at the end of the day.

Navy Admiral William McRaven found YouTube fame when he gave a commencement address to the University of Texas graduating class of 2014. He shared 10 life lessons from his time as a Navy SEAL, but one resonated far more than the others. Admiral McRaven told graduates to make their beds.

"If you make your bed every morning, you will have accomplished the first task of the day. It will give you a small sense of pride, and it will encourage you to do another task, and another, and another. And by the end of the day, that one task completed will have turned into many tasks completed. Making your bed will also reinforce the fact that the little things in life matter. If you can't do the little things right, you'll never be able to do the big things right. And if by chance you have a miserable day, you will come home to a bed that is made."

While the admiral gave good reasons for making your bed, he neglected a very important one that's supported by research:

Willpower is a transferable skill.

Psychologists Meg Oaten and Ken Cheng recruited some people who wanted to improve their physical fitness, some others who wanted better study habits, and a third group who wanted to better manage their money. All participants received immediate help setting goals and planning. Members of each group were asked to keep a log of their workouts, study sessions, and spending. From time to time, the volunteers were asked to come into a lab to perform an exercise that required close concentration. To test their self-control, the researchers placed a television screen showing an Eddie Murphy stand-up routine within view. In order to complete the boring concentration task, participants had to use willpower to ignore Eddie Murphy's jokes.

As time passed, the people who regularly exercised self-control by working out, forcing themselves to study, and resisting the urge to spend got progressively better at ignoring Murphy's act and performed better for longer periods of time on the concentration task. They also made progress on their goals. The athletes were fitter, the studiers got more schoolwork done, and the spendthrifts saved more money. But they also improved in other areas, and this is the lesson teachers can take from Admiral McRaven's advice to make your bed. Those who were trying to study more also ended up exercising more often. The people who wanted to manage their money more responsibly reported studying more often. On the whole, participants in all three groups smoked fewer cigarettes, drank less alcohol, ate less junk food, and kept a cleaner house that they had previously. Some even reported better control over their tempers.

Willpower could be used to strengthen willpower, and willpower gains in one area led to willpower gains in other areas.

Making your bed is a task that requires self-discipline, and forcing yourself to do it every day builds willpower. That willpower carries over into other, more consequential areas of your life. There's nothing magical about making your bed. You can establish any simple habit that requires self-discipline. You can force yourself to sit with correct posture, or intentionally change your speech patterns so that your enunciate each sound. You can use self-control to stop biting your nails, or to floss every night. You can call upon self-discipline to stop swearing, or never use sarcasm again.

As a teacher, I'm sure you recognize the applications. By practicing self-control, you can gain more willpower for yourself, but you can also improve your students' self-discipline. Admiral McRaven admits that he didn't understand why making his bed was so important to his superiors while he was going through SEAL training. He didn't appreciate the wisdom of it until much later in life. Similarly, as a child, I never understood what I thought at the time were nitpicky requirements from some of my teachers, but I get it now. As the admiral said, little things matter.

Requiring students to always push in their chairs when they leave their seat might be a good start. Whether or not you care about the appearance of your room at ten o'clock in the morning isn't the point. You're teaching students a habit that requires self-discipline. The research indicates that those students who master this small task will benefit from increased self-control in other areas of their lives. Requiring things like a specific format on the headings of papers, neat handwriting, good posture, and clear diction may feel old-fashioned, but teachers who demand small acts that require self-control may in fact be building more self-disciplined students.

If you're a teacher you've probably heard of Walter Mischel's marshmallow experiment. To quickly summarize, young children were given the option of eating a marshmallow now or delaying gratification with the promise of getting two marshmallows later. Those who were able to hold off for the second marshmallow grew up to lead more successful lives by almost every measure. They had better grades, scored higher on the SAT, were more popular with their peers, were in better physical condition, made more money as adults, and were less likely to be bald (kidding on that one).

Mischel's experiment is often cited as evidence of the long-term benefits of self-control. What's instructive for teachers hoping to save themselves from exhaustion, however, is *how* the kids were able to resist temptation. This was actually Mischel's main interest. He wanted to see which strategies helped children wait. What worked best wasn't self-control in the way we normally think of it. Children didn't stare at the marshmallow and grit their teeth until the researcher returned with their prize. They distracted themselves. Some turned around and faced the wall. Others covered their eyes with their hands. A few fiddled with their shoelaces. Some looked away and sang.

Out of sight, out of mind. It's a lesson teachers hoping to use less willpower should heed. If you're constantly fighting the urge to check your cellphone during the school day every time you see the blinking notification light, hide the thing and only take it out at predetermined times.

If you frequently fight off the temptation to partake in the delicious donuts your well-meaning (but ultimately evil) co-workers place in the teachers' lounge, then distract yourself by walking past the lounge without looking in or take a route that doesn't go by the lounge at all.

If Timmy is picking his nose and you're tempted to tell him how gross he's being, stop looking at Timmy. It might not be in any teacher training courses, but sometimes you just have to walk away or direct your attention elsewhere.

Elementary teachers are masters at this. Instead of saying, "Steven, get your hands out of your desk! I've told you ten times already!" they turn to angelic Sarah and say, "Sarah, I really like the way you have your hands folded in front of you." This kind of language is often criticized as manipulative. It's also a bit passive-aggressive. But it will help you keep your cool and focus on positives instead of negatives.

Instead of using willpower to fight off the urge to snap at Steven, simply notice something else that requires less willpower. While you could follow the marshmallow kids' example and sing to yourself, you can also distract yourself by thinking of other things. When you feel yourself fighting the urge to say something critical, think instead of your weekend plans, your planned spring break vacation, or the glass of wine (or *glasses* of wine) you'll drink after work.

Postponing can also be effective. People who tell themselves "not now, but later," are generally less tormented by the temptation of something they are trying to avoid. If your principal says something during a staff meeting that you'd like to forcefully rebut, telling yourself, "not now, but later," will prevent you from fighting to repress those harsh comments in a public forum. Postponing your criticism by telling yourself that you'll write the principal a calm and respectful email after school will help you move past it and conserve willpower. You'll be able to refocus on your job. Once time has passed, you'll likely find that your frustration has abated. This tactic will allow you to avoid an unnecessary conflict that damages your relationship with your boss, which will aid you in managing stress at work.

It takes a lot of willpower to suppress your personality, beliefs, and natural inclinations. If you like to joke around and be silly, it will take self-control for you to be serious at work. If you believe state report cards of schools and principal evaluations of teachers are largely meaningless, it will take willpower to hold your tongue during a meeting at which an administrator is trying to persuade you to care about either. If your natural inclination when criticized is to strike back, you will exhaust your store of willpower by suppressing that instinct when your methods are questioned by another teacher.

Psychologist Mark Muraven and his team found that people who exert self-control to please others were more depleted than people who held true to their own internal goals and desires. It may make you more likable and less likely to get fired, but when it comes to willpower, people-pleasers are at a disadvantage.

Instead of suppressing your emotions and desires, you need to release them. But you can't go around telling off Joyce for leaving a mess in the staff lounge microwave, and you can't respond to your principal's newest idea with your honest opinion because your honest opinion is that his idea is dumb. Here's what you can do:

I sometimes receive an email from a parent or supervisor that angers me. My instinct is to return fire. That's a bad instinct, but that doesn't mean I have to hold in those feelings. It also doesn't mean I should vent to other teachers or my wife. They've got their own problems, and nobody really wants to hear mine. What I do instead is write my honest, no-holds-barred rebuttal. I let it all out, hammering the keyboard and plastering my screen with vitriol. I read it and reread it until it effectively conveys the righteous indignation I so strongly feel.

Then I don't send it.

It releases my anger, and it's there for me to revisit. On those few occasions when I have gone back to reread these unsent missives, my anger is gone. I wonder why I was so outraged at the time. They're actually kind of embarrassing to read. If you do this a few times, you begin to realize that your initial feelings are often an overreaction (and maybe also the result of depleted willpower and low blood sugar) and it becomes easier to avoid indulging them. With time, you'll train yourself to recognize that what you feel in the heat of the moment is not what you will feel when you've cooled off, and this will help put your feelings in proper perspective.

Sometimes, despite careful planning and our best efforts, we just have a day. Life happens, and not everything can be prepared for. On such days, the amount of willpower we use will dramatically reduce our blood sugar levels. We'll be more likely to make decisions we'll later regret. In one study, glucose levels were measured in 107 married couples over 21 days. To measure aggressive impulses, each evening participants stuck between 0 and 51 pins into a voodoo doll that represented their spouse, depending how angry they were with them. To measure aggression, participants competed against their spouse on a 25-trial task in which the winner blasted the loser with loud noise through headphones. As expected, the lower the level of glucose in the blood, the greater number of pins participants stuck into the voodoo doll, and the higher intensity and longer duration of noise participants set for their spouse.

So if you're depleted and unable to eat or sleep, avoid making big decisions before meals. It's when you haven't eaten for a number of hours or are low on sleep that you're at greatest risk of succumbing to the negative effects of low willpower. Meetings after school are a bad idea. Everyone in the room is running on fumes and tempers can easily flare. Decisions made at these meetings have a greater chance of being ill-considered, as depleted teachers and administrators suffering from decision fatigue lack the energy to consider trade-offs. They'll be more likely to go with the easiest choice instead of the best one. Hold meetings in the morning or feed everyone before starting in on the agenda.

When you're sick, stay home. Your body responds to illness by directing glucose to your immune system, leaving your brain (and the rest of your body) with less. You won't be a very good teacher when you're sick. You'll be in a sour mood, prone to poor decisions, and you'll respond more emotionally than usual. Suck it up and write the sub plans. Stay home, get better, and if your spouse says something nasty to you, take it out on your voodoo doll.

Automate Decisions

"Automation is good, so long as you know exactly where to put the machine."

Eliyahu Goldratt

The writer Haruki Murakami once explained his daily routine:

"When I'm in writing mode for a novel, I get up at 4:00 am and work for five to six hours. In the afternoon, I run for 10km or swim for 1500m (or do both), then I read a bit and listen to some music. I go to bed at 9:00 pm. I keep to this routine every day without variation. The repetition itself becomes the important thing."

Deciding is difficult and depleting. The more routines you have, the fewer decisions you need to make and the less tired you will be. Like Murakami, the more teachers can put their work days on cruise control, the more energy they'll have at the end of them.

Teaching is, at its core, the act of making decisions. We decide what to do and what our students will do. We decide which students can work together, and which should be kept apart. We decide when to teach what and how much time to spend on it. We decide how to deliver content, how to encourage participation, how to help struggling learners, and how students should be expected to behave in our classrooms. We develop plans and contingencies for when those plans fail. We design rules and procedures to maximize learning and ensure an efficiently run classroom. Then we decide on interventions and consequences for when those rules are broken and procedures aren't followed. We decide how to respond to student requests, questions, complaints, personal problems, successes, and failures. We decide how to interact with colleagues, bosses, and parents. We decide what to grade and how to grade it.

Making decisions when you're a teacher is unavoidable. As a leader, it's up to you to chart a course, motivate others to follow you, and respond when they don't. Good decisions lead to successful relationships, productive days, and fulfilling careers. Bad decisions can lead to misery. Teachers need to be able to make good decisions, and to do that they need to make fewer of them.

There's a good reason Mark Zuckerberg wears the same gray T-shirt to work every day. It's not because he's a slob. He simply understands decision fatigue. He explains:

"I really want to clear my life to make it so that I have to make as few decisions as possible about anything except how to best serve this community."

President Obama understood the draining effects of deciding, too. He explained his wardrobe this way:

"You'll see I wear only gray or blue suits. I'm trying to pare down decisions. I don't want to make decisions about what I'm eating or wearing, because I have too many other decisions to make."

Jeff Bezos says:

"When you're talking about decisions, quality is usually more important than quantity."

Steve Jobs, Henry Rollins, Christopher Nolan, and even Albert Einstein later in life all subscribed to the same belief. They knew that the more decisions they made, the more tired they would be and the less energy they would have to make important decisions later in the day.

Choosing your outfit is one decision you can easily remove from your day. If you don't want to go the Zuckerberg route, condense all of your decisions into one 15-minute block on a Sunday night when you select your outfits for the entire week. Alternatively, you could choose tomorrow's outfit the night before, which will effectively remove a series of decisions from the start of each day.

Most of us follow the same route to work and back every day. We don't decide; we just do it. The same goes for nearly all of our morning routines. In fact, if you're like me, you're bothered when the customary patterns of your morning get thrown off for some reason.

When you automate a routine, you're forming a habit. In his book, *The Power of Habit*, Charles Duhigg breaks habits down into three components. Understanding these components will help you establish new habits so you can make fewer decisions.

The first part of a habit is the trigger, or cue. The trigger is what tells your body to start doing the thing we think of as a habit. You feel anxious, so you bite your nails. You get dressed in the morning, then automatically brush your teeth. You get home from work and immediately wash your hands and change your clothes.

The second part of a habit loop is the thing you do, the routine. This is what you try to change when you "break a habit." It's the new action you want to take when you establish a new habit. It's what you train students to do as part of your classroom routines.

The third part of a habit loop is the reward. Biting my nails relieves some of my anxiety. Brushing my teeth makes me feel ready to go out into the world. Washing my hands and changing my clothes removes the feeling of school and symbolizes a shift from work time to personal time.

Once habits are ingrained, you perform routines *without thinking*. That's what makes them habits. Therefore, if you want to make fewer conscious decisions during the day, set up more habits.

As a teacher, you instinctively know this. It's why you have classroom procedures. You don't want students coming to you every morning and asking where to put completed homework, so you establish a procedure at the start of the year. Students have to remind themselves of the procedure for the first few weeks, but if they successfully execute it enough times it becomes a habit, something they do without conscious thought.

Many teachers use triggers to initiate their routines. My daughter's third grade teacher played a song — the same song every day — for the routine of moving students through math stations. When students heard the song begin, they knew all the steps they needed to take. Very little decision-making was needed. Students could conserve the energy they would have used deciding what they needed, where to go, and what to do for more important tasks, like learning math.

The rewards for following such routines are many. Something gets accomplished. There are fewer conflicts. Students avoid having the teacher make them do the procedure over again. There's the satisfaction of doing something correctly and efficiently. There's often praise from the teacher or even some tangible reward if it's a mindless, unmotivating task like cleaning up the room at the end of the day.

Everything you do to establish routines for your students you can do for yourself to limit the number of decisions you make. Habits are your brain's way of conserving energy. Think of how exhausting it would be if you had to consciously decide those things you automatically do every day. Should you shampoo your hair first or wash your face? Which side of the bed will you sleep on tonight? Should you use a fork for the mashed potatoes or a spoon?

Start by making a list of the things you often do. Then see which ones can be automated. Instead of going to the gym and deciding which equipment to use and what order to use it in, just do the same workout routine every time or follow a predetermined rotation. Don't decide what to have for dinner every day. Instead, use your limited decision-making energy to plan your meals for the entire week. Now eating dinner becomes a thoughtless matter of simply following your plan. Analyze every part of your day and eliminate as many decisions as possible by establishing routines.

Since many of the decisions you make at work happen in response to student misbehavior, an effective classroom management plan is a must for teachers wishing to go home with more energy. It can prevent problems that will require decisions from you, and when executed dispassionately, can prevent you from experiencing the high-intensity emotions that stress our bodies. If consequences are clear and consistently enforced, there is no decision to make. You simply follow your predetermined plan.

As with willpower, you'll want to make decisions early so you won't have to make them later. If students know exactly what to do because you established rock-solid routines, modeled them, and had students practice them until they became habits, then you'll have fewer decisions to make throughout the year. How many of the decisions you make in the classroom are already part of a routine, and how many more could be with some simple, proactive changes?

Automate your schedule by making it the same every day, plan units ahead of time, prepare units over the summer when you're well-rested. Use resources that require less decision-making from you. All these can cut the number of decisions you make.

Another way to remove decision-making is to establish rules for yourself. These are your non-negotiables; the things you must simply do. There's no choice in the matter. The author Raymond Chandler had a simple rule to motivate himself to write on those days when he didn't feel like it:

"The important thing is that there should be a space of time, say four hours a day at the least, when a professional writer doesn't do anything but write. He doesn't have to write, and if he doesn't feel like it, he shouldn't try. . . . But he is not to do any other thing,

not read, write letters, glance at magazines . . . . Two very simple rules, a: you don't have to write. b: you can't do anything else. The rest comes of itself."

You're already doing this with parts of your life. If you're like most drivers today, you probably put on your seatbelt without even thinking about it. You made it a rule for yourself. Now it's a habit you don't even think about. Some people have rules for their diets, like no soda or no eating after a certain time. By making a few rules to follow at school, you can automate parts of your work day. Some of the rules I set for myself include no yelling at my students, always make a to-do list for the next day before I leave school, and never do whole-class punishments. Rules are just decisions you make one time and then commit to, freeing you from making more decisions later on.

A first cousin to establishing rules is to set up default settings for your life. 90% of the time, you open your word processor and use the default font. There's no deciding involved because it suits your purposes almost every time. However, unlike a rule, you allow yourself the flexibility to change should the need arise. You're almost always going to stick with the base setting, but sometimes something else is needed and a decision must be made.

In the classroom, my default answer is no. I try to establish rules and routines at the start of the year that remove as much decision-making as possible, but it's impossible to cover everything. So when students ask permission to do something not explicitly addressed, I almost always say no. If a student asks if she can get something out of her backpack, I usually tell her no. If a student wants to sit at my back table to work, my tendency is to say no. But because no is a setting and not a rule, I allow students to give me reasons and sometimes I say yes. So if the student who wants to sit at the back table explains that her neighbor is distracting her during a test and she thinks she'll work better somewhere else, then I may grant the request.

The saying, "Don't make permanent decisions based on temporary emotions," is good advice. Successful people recognize and understand the intensity of their emotions and the potential those emotions have on their behavior. They train themselves to look at decisions as rationally as possible, taking into account the emotions they're feeling.

Most people are terrible at assessing and managing their emotions. According to one study, just 36 percent of people are able to accurately identify their emotions in the moment. Strong decision-makers, on the other hand, know how bad moods affect them and understand that good moods can be equally dangerous. Understand your own feelings and how they affect your judgments, and you can objectively evaluate the quality of your own decisions.

The best decision-makers use a predetermined set of criteria to weigh their options. They answer the following questions before deciding:

- Is it good for me?
- What are the potential negative effects and how likely are they?
- Will this benefit people I care for?
- How could it hurt those I care for?
- Which choice best reflects my values?
- How will I feel about this decision in the morning? In a month? In five years?

To give just one example, say your principal has asked you to attend an after-school parent night. He wants you to run an informational session for one hour, during which time you will do the same presentation twice. It so happens that this parent night falls on the same night as your daughter's talent show. You're resentful about being asked, and even more resentful about the fact that you won't be paid. You're emotional about the unfairness of it. Your instinct is to tell your principal that it's insulting to expect teachers to donate their nights, but you know that you're emotional and that it's not a good time to make any rash decisions. So you use the above criteria to make a more objective decision.

You decide that although you'll win brownie points from your principal, attending the after-school event is not good for you. There are a few potential negative effects to not going. Your principal might question your dedication and professionalism. Your colleagues might resent your absence. However, attending will not benefit the people you care about most; in fact, it could hurt both your wife and daughter. As for values, you believe that time is the most precious commodity and that you'll never get a second crack at being a father to this daughter. You also believe that because time is precious, you should be paid when acting on behalf of your employer.

How will you feel in the morning? You're likely to feel guilty either way, but you'll feel more guilty if you miss your daughter's talent show. In a month, your colleagues and probably even your principal won't recall which teachers attended the after-school night, but your wife and daughter likely will remember that you chose work over family. You're positive that the memory of watching your daughter sing on stage will still be with you in five years, and equally confident that you won't remember the parent night presentation in five weeks.

Using this criteria, the choice is easy.

90% Calm

"Don't forget to breathe, very important."

Mr. Miyagi
The Karate Kid

I was in a rush to get home the other day, but first I had to stop at the grocery store to pick something up for dinner. As is frequently the case after work, the grocery store was busy and the checkout lines were long. I found what looked to be the shortest line and waited my turn.

Within seconds, I started to notice that the lines on either side of me were moving faster than mine. The lady checking out at the front of my line was paying with a check, I guess because she still lived in the Stone Age. Inevitably, a snag had been hit.

Glancing over my shoulder and seeing a shorter line, I quickly jumped to the next lane. As soon as I did, the matter of the check was resolved and my old line started moving. Still, I stayed put, sure I had made the correct decision. To confirm, I glanced ahead and was dismayed to see the checker had picked up her phone. This is the universal supermarket sign for,

"Something has confused me, and I need help," which meant that there would be a delay while everyone waited for a manager or a more experienced checker to come over.

Why did this always happen to me, and why did it always seem to happen when I was in a hurry?

The story above illustrates two cognitive biases that affect the way we think and make decisions. They're the same two biases that contribute to the belief so many teachers have that in order to be effective, they must expend a lot of energy.

Availability bias is a mental shortcut we use that gives priority to memorable events. It explains why people feel safer driving than flying, why they worry about their kid getting kidnapped, and why most people believe it's more dangerous to be a cop than a garbage man. Our brains assume that easily recalled events occur more frequently. Because plane crashes take over news cycles while car crashes receive little to no coverage, and because a few high-profile child kidnappings dominate cable television even though they're extremely rare, and because whenever a police officer dies in the line of duty it receives a lot of media attention, while we never hear about trash collectors getting clipped by passing motorists, we assume those events we hear about must happen more.

When I'm stuck in line at the supermarket, I quickly recall other times I was in slow-moving lines because the negative emotions associated with those frustratingly slow lines are more memorable than the times when I flew through the line or there was no line at all. I don't remember the numerous times I checked out with no delay. In those instances, I paid no attention to how slowly other lines were moving relative to mine. I only noticed the speed at which my line moved when it wasn't moving as fast as I wanted it to, which was usually when I was in a hurry. It's not that the line I'm in always moves slowly, it's that when I'm in a slow-moving line, I get impatient and frustrated and I'm more apt to remember other times when I felt the same way.

A second bias, confirmation bias, describes our tendency to seek out information that confirms what we already believe. If we think we always end up in the slow line at the supermarket, we'll notice and remember the times our line moves slowly, while ignoring the times it doesn't. When entering a line, we'll seek to confirm our belief that we're moving slowest by comparing our line to ones that are moving faster, and simply not acknowledge (or even look for) lines that are moving slower.

These biases also work to lead teachers to the conclusion that to be effective one must teach with intensity and passion, and that the more you can do that, the more successful you will be. As Americans, we're attracted to showy displays, gusto, and entertainment. Because extroverts attract more attention and are therefore assumed to have greater authority, we teachers believe they are more effective.

The bias for enthusiastic teaching is amplified in our society because most teachers work in obscurity. You can't turn on your television or jump on YouTube and watch a local classroom teacher do her job for a couple of hours. The only teachers we really get to know are the extroverts. They are the ones who branch out and provide professional development, taking the stage for all to see. They present at teacher conferences. They write books and make videos. They're active on social media. Because they're the most outgoing of us, they get noticed more.

If someone asks you to think of an effective teacher, chances are you'll think of a dynamic one because of availability bias. Those teachers are memorable. But if this were a scientific study of teaching methods, it would be unreliable because of selection bias. The teachers we're most aware of are the ones that want people to be aware of them. Bombarded by the same message from those most eager to spread it, teachers start to believe that there is only one way to be a great teacher. We have to act like we're on a stage. We have to perform with vim and vigor. It needs to look like we're working really hard! We must teach with intensity! We need to entertain! We're unable to balance this view because we have few opportunities to observe other kinds of effective teaching.

Confirmation bias perpetuates the belief that the only way to be an effective teacher is to be consistently enthusiastic. Since we receive this message frequently, and since the examples of good teaching that most readily come to mind are those who are enthusiastic, we believe there is a relationship between the two. And because we believe it, we seek out and remember examples that confirm our belief, while at the same time dismissing examples that don't comport with what we already think. We look for examples of effective, energetic teachers and ignore examples of effective teachers who are more reserved. The other side of that coin is that we conveniently forget about animated teachers who aren't very good.

To challenge the cognitive biases that can lead us to believe things that may be untrue, we must first recognize we have them. To combat confirmation bias, we have to admit that we have beliefs, and that those beliefs focus our attention on things we already believe to the exclusion of things we don't. To battle availability bias, we must actively seek out information that's harder to notice. We have to recognize that our brains are efficient, and as an energy-saving tactic they filter out most of what happens to us and present only the most memorable moments, usually those attached to strong feelings. In determining the "best way to teach," we should search out and observe many different teaching styles and be honest in our assessments.

Because we don't often have the opportunity to watch real teachers do real teaching, a more representative sample of teachers might be found by observing athletic coaches. Coaching is teaching, and since sports are so popular in this country, you can turn on your TV at just about any time of the day and see a coach in action. Outwardly passionate coaches are on just as often as more unassuming ones (although the cameras tend to find the mercurial types more frequently).

Like teachers, the most histrionic coaches get the ink. They get noticed. They get interviewed. When they retire, they get jobs on TV. They practically demand attention. They gesticulate wildly on the sidelines, stomping their feet, shouting at both their own players and the referees. Fans cheer their passion and intensity. It mirrors their own zeal for the home team. It's obvious how much these coaches care.

But a fair accounting has to admit that these types of coaches don't have a monopoly on success. Many fail miserably. The volatile Ozzie Guillen was voted the least respected manager in a 2012 players' poll and has been unable to land another managerial job in Major League Baseball despite winning a World Series in 2005. P.J. Carlesimo was a screamer for years on NBA sidelines. No one would question his passion or enthusiasm. But he had a career record of 204-296, and is best known for choking one of his players. College basketball coach Tom Crean is a bundle of frenetic energy on the sidelines. He paces back and forth like a maniac, points, yells, claps, pumps his fists, and sometimes gets down in a defensive stance. Indiana University fired him in 2017 after he failed to make the NCAA tournament in five of his nine years at what used to be a perennial powerhouse of a program.

On the other hand, there are countless calm coaches who have had extraordinary success. The NFL's Tony Dungy and Tom Landry were famous for their cool demeanors, both in practice and in games. Both won Super Bowl rings and are enshrined in their sport's Hall of Fame. Legendary basketball coaches John Wooden, Lenny Wilkens, and Phil Jackson were all reserved on the sideline. Wooden, as calm a coach as there ever was, won 10 NCAA national championships in 12 years at UCLA and is considered one of the best coaches of all time.

Lenny Wilkens was inducted into the NBA Hall of Fame as both a player and a coach. A 1979 *New York Times* article about him said, "In contrast to those who kick over chairs and hurl invectives at officials, the 41-year old Wilkens likes to stand with his arms folded, his lips pursed, and his face expressionless."

Wilkens himself said, "Yelling and screaming is not my nature. I try to get through to my players in other ways."

One of his players, Paul Silas, who would later go on to coach in the NBA himself, said, "Lenny is a very, very, low-key guy. Nothing ever seems to excite him."

Phil Jackson is arguably the most successful coach to ever live. He won 11 NBA titles with the Bulls and Lakers and managed some of the largest egos in the game's history. Jackson earned the nickname "zen master," because of his studies of Eastern philosophies and his use of mindfulness with his players. Instead of shouting, Jackson taught his players to meditate. His approach to pregame rituals illustrates Jackson's coaching philosophy and separates him from many coaches who use the moments before tip-off to shout encouragement to their charges. Jackson said, "There's only so much a player can absorb when his body is pulsing with adrenaline. This is not a good time for deep left-brain discussions. It's the moment to calm the player's minds and strengthen their spiritual connection with one another before they head into battle."

If you still doubt that a calm teacher can be as effective as an energetic one, consider that other cultures have very different values from the west — cultures that stress the importance of mindfulness, quiet, and inner peace — and their students regularly outperform Americans on international exams.

Overtly enthusiastic people are not the only ones who succeed. Many styles work. You have to do what fits your personality. If your colleague is high-octane, you don't have to be, and just because a lot of "famous" teachers happen to be high-energy types doesn't mean that's the only path to success.

A 1983 study by researchers at the University of Southern Mississippi and the University of Georgia found no effect of teacher enthusiasm on the achievement of fourth grade students in social studies. Researchers did, however, observe increased classroom management problems in the classrooms led by high-enthusiasm teachers. In another study, also done in 1983, students taught by teachers trained to deliver lessons with high enthusiasm learned no more than students taught the same content by teachers who taught with their natural teaching style. Once again, students taught by the high-enthusiasm teachers exhibited more off-task behavior than their peers. A 2012 study of three- and four-year olds concluded that there were no significant achievement differences between students taught in a low, medium, or highly enthusiastic manner.

Students tend to reflect their teachers. Calm teachers lead to calm classes, and calm classes allow for more focused work and less excitability. When was the last time you tried to concentrate while feeling intense emotion? It's not easy. In fact, brain-imaging research shows that when we experience intense emotions, our amygdalas activate, setting off the body's stress response. It's the job of the prefrontal cortex to tell our amygdalas to cool their jets when the threat isn't real. But while it's busy doing that, it's unable to engage in higher-order thinking, such as reasoning, logic, problem-solving, planning, and memory that we need to learn.

Think of the last time you learned something new. Did you pump yourself up with some AC/DC? Of course not. An elevated heart rate might be helpful before a football game, but it's not all that useful if you're trying to learn Portuguese.

Staying calm leads to better self-control. People who are calm have the ability to choose their actions instead of reacting emotionally. If you think of the worst decisions of your life, they were likely made when you were experiencing high-intensity emotions. By staying calm, teachers can react to anything that happens in their classrooms in a way they won't later regret. When Anton shoves a straw up his nostril again, they'll be calm enough to say, "Throw the straw away, please," and not "For Christ's sake, Anton, how many times do I have to tell you to stop sticking straws up your damn nose!?"

It's sometimes easy to forget that we're role models and that are students are always watching. When we seesaw back and forth between high-intensity emotions, and when we react emotionally to events around us, we are modeling to students that it is acceptable for them to do the same. How many times have you told a student to think before they acted? Take your own advice.

I'm not suggesting that teachers never show emotion. I'm recommending that we deploy emotions strategically for maximum effect. There are times when we need to be intense to get students' attention or to get them excited about a lesson. Nor should we temper our authentic enthusiasm for topics we're genuinely excited about; that's one of the joys of teaching. But there are other times — *most times* — when calm is better. When you intentionally use emotion, you remain in control, and because you're rarely emotional, you'll have more impact when you are.

The biggest reason to stay calm is your own energy. Remember, high-intensity emotions can drain us. Exhausted teachers make mistakes, which adds stress to their days. They lack the energy they need to be effective, which increases their frustration. They have trouble being patient when things go wrong and damage relationships with students, which makes it even harder to maintain calm in the classroom. Exhausted, stressed out, and frustrated, many of them burn out, and burned out teachers are far, far worse than calm ones.

So how do you stay calm? Try these strategies:

Calm Morning Rituals

Many people wake up as late as possible and rush through their mornings, starting their days with stressful sprints to get showered, dressed, out of the house, and on the road, where they simultaneously try to eat, suck down their first coffee, find a good song on satellite radio, and dart in and out of traffic to get to work on time. A calmer approach would be to get up earlier and ease into your day. You might start with a little meditation and a few yoga poses. Morning is a great time to write or to exercise. A calm, leisurely breakfast will fill your glucose tank and prepare you for the day. Try to get to school early, giving yourself plenty of time to prepare. Prepared people are confident, and confident people are calm and in control.

Precommitment

George Washington famously said, "I cannot tell a lie." I don't know if Washington ever lied or not (he probably told Martha she looked good in a dress, and having seen portraits of Martha, that might be stretching the truth), but I'll wager he didn't lie very often. Once stated so publicly, honesty became a part of his identity. Teachers can use the same trick.

Decide ahead of time that nothing is going to ruffle your feathers. You're not going to get overly excited or upset no matter what happens. Like Washington, make this trait a part of who you are. Talk it up. Print it out and hang it by your desk. Develop a mantra to remind yourself. Commit yourself to this new version of you. The declaration will make you accountable because you won't want to feel like a hypocrite. Consistency is a powerful influence on people's behavior. Use it to your advantage.

When I was trying to lose weight, one simple thing I decided to do was drink less soda. I'd read that if I didn't drink pop for a whole year, I could lose 15 pounds without making any other changes. That seemed easy enough. I didn't love soda anyway, and drinking water would have the added bonus of saving me money. So I made myself a rule: No Pop. I avoided soda by never buying it at the grocery store, so I didn't have it in the house. Unlike John Edwards, I removed the temptation. When I went out to eat, I ordered water. This was easy because I'm cheap. Not buying soda saved me at least a dollar every meal. The only place where my No Pop rule was a challenge was when I ordered fast food. Because I tend to order value meals, I pay for the soda whether or not I get a soda. In this case, my thrift worked to my disadvantage. If I was paying for it, then I should get it. I had to make a new rule: No Fast Food. I eventually ended up with a list of rules for myself, many of which are described in my first book, *The Teacher's Guide to Weight Loss*. When I follow these rules, I lose weight. If you follow your rules for conserving willpower, you'll end up with more energy. And most teachers like to follow rules.

Visualize

Morris Goodman was one of the best insurance agents in the world when he crashed his brand new Cessna at age 35. With his neck broken, his spinal cord crushed, and every major muscle in his body destroyed, Morris was no longer able to perform any bodily function except to blink his eyes. Doctors told him he would never walk or even be able to breathe without a respirator again. His body ruined but his mind still intact, Morris relentlessly visualized himself walking out of the hospital. Eight months later, that's just what he did. Doctors had no explanation, but Morris did. "A man becomes what he thinks about," he said.

If you want to respond calmly during the school day, be like Morris Goodman. Visualize yourself doing the thing you want to do. See yourself responding calmly. Write down the situations that typically trigger an emotional response from you. Do you flip your lid over dishonesty? Do you snap at students who blurt out while you're teaching? Does a loud and sloppy transition leave you seeing red? List them all.

Keep your list near your desk. Before students arrive each morning, read it through and visualize yourself handling those moments coolly and confidently. See yourself responding with poise and calmly enforcing consequences. Picture yourself following through, reteaching, modeling, and resetting expectations.

Visualization has been shown to be nearly as effective as actual practice. An Australian psychologist named Alan Richardson once gathered together a group of students to shoot some free throws. He then split the group into three. One group would practice free throws for 20 minutes each day. A second group would only visualize themselves making free throws for 20 minutes each day. The third group did nothing. After four weeks, the participants were tested again. Those who had done nothing didn't get any better or worse. Those who had practiced improved by 24 percent. The visualizers who had only picked up a ball in their imaginations improved by 23 percent. Visualization works, and it's a powerful technique to use when trying to learn a new skill, such as staying calm in the midst of stressful situations.

Simplify

Go anywhere there are people and count how many of them are multi-tasking. It's an epidemic. They text while riding the subway, while walking, and even while driving. They eat while perusing social media. They work with the TV on. They plan their days while doing chores. They listen to a podcast while working out. They try to have a conversation while still thinking about the Facebook post they just saw.

Trying to do more than one thing at a time is a great way to cause a level of anxiety that runs through everything you do because you're always worried you should be doing more, or doing something else. Try just doing one thing. Just eat. Just walk. Just converse. Just write. Just read your email, one at a time. There's peace in giving your full attention to a single activity.

It's difficult to do as a teacher because we have so much to do, but simplifying can calm your mind and allow for greater productivity. Just grade papers. Just meet with one student at a time. Just listen to what a student is telling you without worrying about what the rest of the class is up to. Just sit down and plan one lesson, all the way through.

Reduce noise

Our lives are filled with all kinds of noise — visual clutter, notifications, office announcements, social media, emails demanding to be read. Most of it is unnecessary. Keep your cell phone in your desk and only take it out a couple of times per day. Hit the Do Not Disturb button on your work phone to cut down on interruptions in class. Give some of your stuff away. Be sure there are moments of your day where students are expected to work quietly and independently, both to improve their self-reliance and problem-solving, but also to create moments of quiet for yourself. Reduce the noise, and create some peace in your classroom.

Be Self-Aware

Being outwardly calm won't do you any good if you're a boiling cauldron of emotions on the inside. This kind of self-control will tire you even more than displaying the emotions you're feeling. To conserve energy, you must actually feel calm. To start, regularly monitor your emotions at work. *How am I feeling right now? How's my heart rate? Am I calm? Do I feel edgy? Am I tired and irritable?* Make it a challenge and see how calm you can be. When a student misbehaves, that's when you force yourself to remain calm. A lot of the time, your seeming lack of interest will help de-escalate the situation. Learn to watch your response. When something stressful happens, what do you do? Some people jump into action. Others get angry, or overwhelmed. Still others start to feel sorry for themselves, and wish things were different. They engage in self-pity and wonder why people can't behave better. Monitor your reactions, because they're often habits. If you find a bad one, use what you know about habit loops to replace it with a better one.

Many teachers take things personally. If someone does something they don't like, they interpret it as a personal affront. Students who aren't working are defying them! Students who fail to say thank you don't appreciate them! A student who responds disrespectfully to a reasonable request is trying to ruin their day! Some teachers seem to think the universe itself is out to get them. But the truth is, it's rarely personal. High school principal David Geurin says, "A student's behavior usually says far more about what they are going through than what they are trying to put you through." So stop making everything about you. It's almost assuredly not.

Slow Down

The body follows the mind, but the mind also follows the body. You can feel happier by forcing yourself to smile. You can feel calmer by taking deep breaths. You can feel more assertive by widening your stance, standing up straight, and placing your hands on your hips. You can boost your confidence by holding your arms aloft in a victory pose. You can feel more alert by sitting up straight.

Even the way we walk impacts our state of mind. In one experiment, a group of participants was trained to walk with a straight back and elastic, light steps, what the researchers labeled a "happy" walk. A second group was trained to walk with hanging shoulders and heavy steps, an "unhappy" walk. A camera and a computer measured how happy or unhappy their walks were. Afterwards, volunteers were presented with lists of both positive and negative words, such as *beautiful* and *ugly*, and were asked to write down the words they remembered best. The results showed that the participants who had walked happily were able to recall more positive words, whereas the participants with unhappy walks mostly recalled negative words. Our posture not only influences how we feel, but also determines what information we pay attention to and remember the most.

It follows then that teachers who want to be calmer in the classroom can do so by slowing down. Speak slower and move slower. Do everything at a more languid pace. Calm your body and your mind will follow. This doesn't mean that you have to move in slow motion or in any way that is obvious to your students. Just ease up on your pace a bit and your breathing will deepen, your muscles will relax, and you will begin to feel more at peace.

Your cool demeanor might even rub off on your students. Students often reflect their teachers' moods, so your composure has the potential to spread from one student to the next and fill your classroom with a feeling of serenity.

Whenever you feel anything other than calm, take a deep breath and engage in self-talk. Try using perspective. Ask yourself, "Is this worth getting upset about?" Or, "In the grand scheme of things, does this really matter?" Or remind yourself that in just three more hours you'll be home with a beer in your hand. You can also tell yourself that responding emotionally will likely backfire, if not in the short term with students who engage you in a shouting match and other power struggles, then in the long term with deteriorating relationships.

Classroom Management Plan

The best thing you can do for your own emotions is have a classroom management plan that students understand and that you consistently follow. When students misbehave, the plan tells you what to do. You don't need to make decisions, and there's no reason to be emotional. When a student breaks a rule, your job is to act as a referee and make the call. Just deliver the predetermined consequence and move on.

Do Less

If you're finding that despite your best intentions of staying calm, you're in front of the class doing your little song and dance and trying to motivate and inspire students with your instruction, then you may be too central to your classroom. Stop needing to be the star of the show. Keep lessons short and focused on one learning goal. If you're talking for longer than 15 minutes, you've likely lost some of your audience anyway. Step back, and turn the stage over to your students. Get them doing more while you recede into the shadows.

Teach students how to work, and expect them to do so. Don't jump in to give hints or rescue students from failure. Let them struggle and devise their own coping strategies to get back on track. Do less, and require them to do more. Keep at it, and you'll do them the favor of combatting the learned helplessness teachers see in so many young people today.

Train a few "coaches on the floor." You may be the expert in the room, but if the only people we could learn from were experts, then we'd be in a lot of trouble as a species. You have students in your room who know more than other students. Put them to work by having them help their classmates. Many times, kids learn better from other kids than from adults.

You have three jobs:

- Teach the content in the most engaging way possible, but keep it short.

- Put students to work and stay out of their way, observing them and taking notes on what you'll need to do next.

- Provide feedback in the moment on the work they've done. Let them know how they're progressing toward the learning goals.

Stepping back will empower your students, and it will allow you to go home with more energy. You don't have to do it all. Stay calm, and trust your students.

Taming the Terrible Master

"A man is what he thinks about all day long."

Ralph Waldo Emerson

The actor Chris Pratt dropped out of community college halfway through his first semester. He worked as a discount ticket salesman for a while, then as a daytime stripper. Eventually, a friend invited him to live in Maui, where he ended up homeless, spending his nights sleeping in a van or in a tent on the beach. Not especially motivated, he took a part-time job as a waiter at a Bubba Gump Shrimp Co. One day, he waited on a woman named Rae Dawn Chong. She was a little-known actress who was making a short film. Impressed by Pratt's attitude, she offered him a part. That opportunity led to two years as a struggling actor in Los Angeles, then a dozen more years as Pratt clawed his way to the top of his profession. He eventually landed a breakout role in the television show *Parks and Recreation*, and then starred in blockbuster movies like *Guardians of the Galaxy* and *Jurassic World*. In 2016, Chris Pratt earned $26 million and was Hollywood's second most bankable star.

What was it about a homeless, aimless, part-time waiter's attitude that caught the attention of Chong and led to the opportunity that would turn Pratt's life around? *Men's Health* called it "positive without being overzealous." Chris Pratt is fun to be around, a characteristic that seems to come naturally to him but is actually the result of a deliberate decision.

Pratt says, "Your attitude is a choice. Real fun – there's no choice in that. But at other times, when it feels like it's down to you whether or not you enjoy yourself? I'm lucky in that it's easier for me to get a kick at work than it is for a lot of people. Even so, it's important to me to behave like that. It's how I was raised. Are you going to leave people feeling good? It's about understanding that your attitude is contagious and asking yourself if it's worth catching."

Even when he was sleeping in a van in Hawaii, Pratt found the bright side. "It's a pretty awesome place to be homeless," he said. It's that positivity that caught the attention of Rae Dawn Chong. People are attracted to optimism.

Having a positive attitude involves nothing more than making an intentional decision to see the world differently. People like Chris Pratt train themselves to look at the positive side of things instead of the negative. Rather than regretting the decision to fly to Hawaii without any job prospects, you realize that there are far worse places to be a bum. Psychologists call this *reframing*. Chris Pratt is a master of it. Nearly everything he says and does is upbeat.

Every one of us chooses our attitude every second of every day.

Each year, I ask my students to think of a person they know who is seemingly always in a good mood. Then I ask them to think of someone who always seems to be grumpy. Then I ask them, "Do you really think one person's life is that much better than the other person's?"

If you're a teacher living in America, chances are your life is far more similar to other teachers than different. You have a roof over your head, enough food to eat, a way to get to the places you need to go, people who love you and whom you love, a job that pays the bills (most of them, anyway). You have a few luxuries, like some nice pairs of shoes, an Amazon Prime membership, maybe a Keurig. And yet how widely do the attitudes of the teachers you know vary? I imagine you can easily think of a colleague who never has anything good to say just as easily as you can think of one who lights up the room with positivity when she enters.

Two people can be in the exact same place experiencing the exact same thing and have complete polar reactions based on nothing but their attitudes. Your experience is entirely your creation. Wouldn't you rather it be a happy one?

Acceptance

Part of staying positive is accepting that which we cannot change. This past August we started school on the day of a solar eclipse. The entire school planned to go outside to watch it. Then, about two hours before the big event, we received an email explaining that a ball had been dropped and there were no eclipse glasses in the school. There was not a thing I could do about it, so there was no point in getting upset. Instead, I used the occasion to model positive thinking for my students. I knew that they would take their cue from me, so I had to sell the fact that this was actually a good thing. I told them that in Michigan, the sun would only be 80 percent eclipsed, but the places on NASA's livestream would reach totality. It would be way cooler to watch it on the SMART Board in my classroom. And, if we watched it on the screen, we'd see *multiple* eclipses.

Acceptance doesn't mean you don't work toward change if change is possible. It means differentiating between things you have some control over and things you don't, then choosing to see the silver lining that always exists if you decide to look for it.

Stop Negative Self-Talk

It's natural to get down on yourself, but self-talk can either perpetuate your negativity or help you get past it. Negative self-talk is self-defeating. It sends you down an emotional spiral that is difficult to pull out of.

Negative people have a tendency to internalize self-criticism by confusing their mistakes as permanent personality traits. Teachers like this might forget to make copies they need for a lesson and respond by thinking, "Uh, I'm so forgetful."

A better approach is to think of your actions as unique to the moment, no matter how often you believe you mess up. When you start treating each situation as its own and stop beating yourself up over every mistake, you'll stop making your problems bigger than they are. Replace judgmental statements like, "I'm so stupid," with factual ones like, "I made a mistake." Give yourself permission to screw up. You're going to. Accept it when it happens, and move on. Attaching a permanent, pejorative label to yourself leaves no room for improvement.

How you respond is always your choice. You can choose to avoid negative thinking that will add to your stress and adopt a more productive mindset instead. Here are a few examples teachers sometimes face:

Situation: You are bored in a meeting.

Negative Thinking: *This is such a waste of time. I have so much to do right now. It's ridiculous that we have to sit through this when everyone knows how crushed teachers are for time.*

Positive Thinking: *Even though this meeting isn't useful to me, I'm going to use this time to pretend to take notes but actually plan next week's lesson plans.*

Situation: You have sent Alexandra to the office three times this week and the principal keeps sending her right back.

Negative Thinking: *My principal is so spineless. He doesn't discipline kids at all. The inmates are running the asylum, and my authority is being undermined every time he fails to follow through!*

Positive Thinking: *Well, I guess I'll handle discipline on my own, which is a good thing because I don't want my students to think anyone is in charge of my room except me.*

Situation: Your principal has just observed your lesson and it did not go well.

Negative Thinking: *I'm doomed! I'm going to get a bad evaluation and be put on an improvement plan. And everybody knows that's what happens right before they get rid of you. I'll probably have to live in my parents' basement.*

Positive Thinking: *That didn't go too well. I'll just admit it and ask my principal if she can come back in sometime in the next couple of weeks to watch a different lesson. And if not, there's nothing I can do about it now except work on the things that need improving. I'll start with reteaching my students how to come to attention when I ask for it.*

Beware the Company You Keep

If you're trying to be a more positive person, then be careful of the company you keep. People's attitudes are contagious. Research from the Department of Biological and Clinical Psychology at Friedrich Schiller University in Germany found that exposure to negative emotional stimuli—including complainers and cynics— caused subjects' brains to have the same emotional reactions that they experienced when stressed. Like stress, the longer you stay in such a situation, the worse off you'll be.

Complainers are bad news because they wallow in their problems and fail to focus on solutions. They want people to join their pity party so that they can feel better about themselves. Teachers often feel pressure to listen to complainers because we don't want to seem callous or rude, but there's a fine line between lending a sympathetic ear and getting sucked into their negativity. You can avoid this by setting limits and distancing yourself when necessary. Think of it this way: If you sat down in a theater and quickly realized the people sitting behind you were loudmouths, would you allow them to ruin your enjoyment of the movie, or would you get up and find a different seat?

A great way to set limits is to ask complainers how they intend to fix the problem. This will either redirect the conversation in a more productive direction or shut them up. At the least, they'll know you're not interested in hearing anymore whining. As the great philosopher Rihanna said, "Don't let the bastards get you down."

Take Control

While acceptance is a positive approach for things outside of your control, many people avoid taking responsibility for things they can do something about. Take charge of the areas of your life that feel out of control, such as your finances, your weight, your relationships, and your attitude, and you'll be a more positive person.

Where you focus your attention determines your emotional state. When you fixate on the problems you're facing, you create and prolong negative emotions and stress. When you focus on actions to better yourself and your circumstances, the self-empowerment will create positive emotions.

Teachers are often given new programs or told to do things that go against their educational beliefs (and sometimes against best practices). Instead of marinating in negativity or complaining and spreading that negativity around, start planning for how to make it work. I know one teacher whose district required teachers to write a learning goal for every lesson they would teach each day. This was time-consuming and stressful for her. But instead of complaining about it or refusing to do it, she accepted that it was something she had to do and figured out a way to appease her principal while keeping her sanity. She wrote vague goals on Monday and just left them up all week. Since administrators only briefly poked their heads into her room, they had no way of knowing.

One of the most frequent forms of negative thinking is worry. You can take control here, too. Start by recognizing worry for what it is: fear of the unknown. Your body will react to worry as if it's a threat, so you have to be the one to tell yourself it isn't.

All worries start with the question, "What if?"

- What if I get fired?
- What if I'm late for the staff meeting?
- What if an angry parent emails my principal?
- What if I get a flat tire on the way to work?
- What if a student refuses to follow any directions?

All worry is fear of what *could* happen.

But lots of things *could* happen. An alien spaceship could land on the playground during recess and abduct a couple of kids, but we don't spend much time worrying about such things.

That's an absurd example but there's a lesson in it. Much of what we worry about is unlikely, some of it *very* unlikely, but we worry anyway. We allow fear to stress us out. We cannot predict the future. We certainly can't control it. That makes worrying about it pointless. The next time you worry, ask yourself two questions:

1. **Is there an actual problem, or is this just something in my head?**

2. **If there is a problem, is there something I can do about it right now?**

If the answer to the second question is yes, then exercise control wherever you can. The mere act of doing something will often ease your concerns. I once had a principal who, when she wanted to meet with me, would say, "Paul, can we schedule a time to talk?" But she wouldn't tell me what she wanted to talk about. Being a normal human with a normal human mind, I always assumed the worst. I'd spend the whole day worrying about it. Inevitably, it would be something unimportant that I needn't have worried about at all. I was stressed out all day over nothing! It would have been far more productive of me to simply ask my principal what she wanted to discuss. When you can exercise control over a situation to relieve your concerns, do so.

Focus on solutions. First, make a list of things you worry about. Put everything you worry about on the list, no matter how small, but don't list anything over which you have no control. For those things, practice acceptance and figure out how to make them work for you.

Now, think of a solution to one of your perceived problems. For example, say you worry about your classroom management. Write that down. Now create a plan to improve. Whatever plan you come up with, the next step is to take action. Start executing your plan. Buy books. Watch videos. Enlist the help of a mentor. Do one thing every day that brings you closer to solving your problem.

Taking action means accepting responsibility for your fears. It puts you in control. Problems won't disappear by themselves, but once you solve one, you'll have the confidence to solve others. When you see that taking control works, you'll be inclined to take positive steps to resolve the other issues in your life that cause you worry. Your worries will affect you less. With a few successes under your belt, you will feel like Marcus Aurelius, who said, "No matter what happens, trust in your ability to address it. Never let the future disturb you. You will meet it, if you have to, with the same weapons of reason which today arm you against the present."

Most of the time, the things we worry about are figments of our imaginations. They're not actual dangers, but doubts. We don't know what will happen, and that bothers us because we tend to assume the most horrific outcomes. It feels threatening, and our bodies, believing we're in danger, initiate the stress response. That's why worrying makes us tired.

It's important to understand that everybody worries. You may know someone who never seems to have a care in the world. But that person worries, too. The difference is in how people *respond* to worry.

It is the relationship the outwardly aloof have with worry that sets them apart from those wracked with anxiety. Those who struggle the most with worry treat it as a danger instead of a doubt. As a result, they treat the symptom with the wrong medicine.

So instead of fighting or fleeing, as you would from a real threat, recognize that doubt is simply a form of discomfort. Treat it as such. When we feel discomfort, we act to alleviate it or we try to relax and let it pass. Do the same with your worries:

1. Acknowledge your discomfort, but recognize that it is not danger. Think: "Huh, I guess I don't know what will happen."

2. Determine whether there is anything you can do to influence the outcome or whether it's out of your control. If you can do something, do it.

3. Remind yourself that most of your past worries never happened and most of your current ones won't either.

In the book, *If You're So Smart, Why Aren't You Happy?*, professor Raj Raghunathan describes something he calls the "Reminisce and Reflect Exercise." He asks his students to recall an intensely negative event from two or more years ago. He then asks them to rank how negative the event was at the time and how negative it is now. Finally, he asks them to rank how "meaningful" they now consider the event to be.

What he's found is that, for most students, negative events lose their sting faster than positive ones lose their shine. Recalling a first kiss provides positive feelings, even many years later, while getting dumped, though excruciating when it happened, is no longer a very painful memory.

The more interesting finding, however, is that past negative events are viewed as much more *meaningful* than past positive events. In fact, the more negative the event, the more meaningful it eventually becomes for the students. That bears repeating:

The more negative the event, the more meaningful it eventually becomes.

That's great news for worriers because it means that even if the very thing you fear comes to pass, you will, at some point in the future, likely cherish its memory. Negative events teach us lessons we don't learn from positive ones. In time, we come to appreciate those things learned at the school of hard knocks. Negative events also make for great stories that we relish telling once the pain of the event has receded. That chair you threw in the classroom led to a lot of problems at the time, but it makes for a good anecdote to include in a book about teacher exhaustion years later.

So when it comes to the things you worry most about, remember: They probably won't happen, but even if they do:

- They won't be as bad as you fear.
- The pain won't last as long as you think.
- You will likely look back on them positively in the future.

Reframe Your Stress

You might remember that teachers report the second highest stress levels on the job of all professions in the U.S., nearly matching that of doctors. But new research shows that it doesn't have to be that way. The negative results of stress, like so much of what makes us tired, is largely in our minds.

In a study of 30,000 adults, participants were asked, "How much stress have you experienced in the last year?" and "Do you believe that stress is harmful for your health?"

People who experienced a lot of stress had a 43 percent higher risk of dying but *only if they believed that stress was harmful to them*. Those who admitted to stress but didn't see it as harmful had the lowest risk of dying of anyone in the study, including those who reported low stress levels. So how can you learn to perceive stress as beneficial instead of harmful? Once again, it starts with reframing.

Instead of thinking of your body's stress response — the pounding heart, fast breathing, tight stomach, and other symptoms you've read so much about in this book — as negative and exhausting, train yourself to see it as a sign that your body is ready for a challenge.

Imagine that you have to give a presentation at a curriculum night. Parents, your colleagues, your principal, and even the Superintendent will be there watching you and you alone at the front of the room. You've got a few minutes before you go on stage, so you read over your notes one last time, praying your laptop, the projector, your slideshow, and the microphone will all work and that the few jokes you stole from the Internet will actually land.

Your hands are clammy, you can hardly catch your breath, and your heart is racing so fast you can feel it in your ears. You say to yourself, *"Oh my god, I'm so nervous. I hate feeling like this. This is terrible. I've gotta get a grip. They'll all see my hands shaking. I'll probably forget everything I planned to say and screw up the punchlines of my purloined jokes."*

At this point, you're well into the negative cycle of stress. Not only are you making failure more likely with this kind of negative self-talk, but this way of thinking about stress actually creates *additional* stress.

To reframe stress, tell yourself a new story:

"Man, I am fired up about this presentation! My body is raring to go. All I have to do is channel this energy into confidence and enthusiasm. Let's do this!"

Those who benefit from stress harness it and make it work for them by believing that it's the body's natural way of preparing them to perform.

So the next time you're experiencing the physical symptoms of stress, stop fighting it. If your breathing is faster, don't try to regulate it — breathe deeper. The extra oxygen will help you think. If your muscles have tightened up, don't strain and make it worse — let the added tension straighten your spine and make you feel strong and tall.

Embrace stress by recognizing it for what it is: a natural response to the situation the body finds itself in. Welcome the feeling, because it means you're about to do some serious living. Instead of stressing about stress, tell yourself, "I need this feeling to do my best." Stress is exhausting a lot of teachers. By changing your perception of it, you can avoid the damaging effects most people believe are inevitable.

Conclusion

Whenever you argue that people should work less, you'll be accused of encouraging laziness. Suggesting that teachers work fewer hours, be less enthusiastic, and go home shortly after dismissal puts one at risk of attracting the wrath of those who believe that teaching is a calling and that we should give all of ourselves to our students without regard for our own well-being.

But the more you work, the less effective you will be.

The more you put on your own plate, the more tired you will get.

The more decisions you make, the more exhausted you will be.

The more self-control you use, the more likely you won't have any left when you need it.

The more responsibility you accept, the more you will worry.

The more you worry, the more stress you will feel.

The more stress you feel, the more tired you will get.

The more tired you get, the more burned out you will become.

The more burned out you become, the more likely it is that you will quit.

And the more good teachers like you quit, the more students will suffer and the worse our education system will be.

If you want to give your best — if you really want to make an impact with kids — start by taking care of yourself. Instead of doing more, do less:

- Work less. Leave shortly after the students.

- Detach at night by taking less work home.

- Take advantage of other people's work to do less planning.

- Use a little willpower early to avoid using a lot later.

- Make fewer decisions by cementing new habits and routines.

- Be less emotional. Maintain an inner calm throughout the day.

- Be less negative. Reframe your thoughts, and take control over your worries and stress.

Taking care of yourself is the best thing you can do for you. But it's also the best thing for your family, your friends, anyone with whom you interact, and your employer. And it's undoubtedly the best thing you can do for your students.

As Cassie Gambler, a first grade teacher in Wyoming, told me:

"You cannot provide your best for students when you are not at your best."

Take care of yourselves, teachers.

Thanks for reading. I hope you enjoyed the book and are able to find ways to be less tired this school year. If you think the book could help other teachers, would you please consider doing the following?

- Tell your teacher friends about *Exhausted.*
- Leave a review of the book at Amazon.com.
- Share the book on your social media accounts.
- Follow Teacher Habits on Facebook and Twitter.
- Subscribe to TeacherHabits.com and forward valuable articles to other teachers.

Thank you.

Acknowledgements

Six months ago, when I was planning this book, I knew I wanted some testimony from real, exhausted teachers. I put out a call through my email list and on Facebook. I am grateful to the teachers who responded. Some of what they told me found its way into this book, and it is better for it. Thank you, teachers, for sharing your frustrations with me.

I would not be writing these books if I didn't have people who wanted to read them. Thank you to the many teachers out there who have read the articles on my blog and bought my books.

I've read a lot of books in my life. I've written very few reviews. They're tricky and time-consuming. So if you have written a review for one of my two previous books, or if you are considering writing a review for this one, I cannot express my gratitude enough. To show my appreciation, I often pull quotes from Amazon reviews and feature them in the "My Books" section of my web site. It's these kind words that often lead to new readers giving the books a chance. Thank you!

Thanks also to my team of proofreaders. The truth is, I don't sell nearly enough books to justify paying a professional to edit my writing. We try to catch them all, but I'm sure we missed a few. I beg your forgiveness. Blame me for any errors; I'm the one who screwed up in the first place.

Thanks to my wife, for her never-ending patience and encouragement. Thanks also to my daughter, Delaney, for feedback on the cover. Also to Mom, Dad, and my brother (and principal), Dave, for their support.

Finally, this book would not have been possible without the hard work of psychologists and those who write about their work. If you'd like to see some of the source material, visit TeacherHabits.com and click on *Exhausted* under the "My Books" tab.

About the Author

Paul Murphy is a third grade teacher in Michigan. This fall, he started his 18th year in the classroom. His writing focuses on improving the lives of teachers, both inside the classroom and out. He enjoys reading, writing, travel, exercise, craft beer, and Cheetos. His feet are perpetually cold, he bites his nails, and he regularly (and almost instinctively at this point) changes the lyrics to songs to make them inappropriate, much to the chagrin of his wife and daughter.

You're still reading?

Why?

Well then, in that case, there are a few good things about him. He does all of his family's grocery shopping, he rarely exceeds his monthly budget, and he's only had two cavities and one speeding ticket in his life.

To read more of his work, visit his website, TeacherHabits.com, or check out his other books on Amazon.

79366880R00107

Made in the USA
Columbia, SC
31 October 2017